Mobil ★★
Travel Guide®

BEIJING

MW00794909

ACKNOWLEDGMENTS

We gratefully acknowledge the help of our representatives for their efficient and perceptive inspections of the lodgings listed. Mobil Travel Guide is also grateful to the talented writers who contributed to this book.

EDITOR
Kim Atkinson

ART DIRECTOR
Julia Brabec

PHOTO EDITOR
Gillian Nadel

WRITERS
Anne Lee, David Black,
Kim Atkinson, Anna Roufos,
Hillary Brylka

RESEARCHER
Mai Hoang

COPY EDITOR
Paula L. Fleming

PRODUCTION DIRECTOR
Mary Connelly

COVER PHOTOS: Kinabaloo.com (1-3),
XIN ZHU/iSTOCKPHOTO

ISBN: 9-780841-60323-3
Manufactured in Canada

10 9 8 7 6 5 4 3 2 1

CONTENTS

pg 30

pg 19

pg 56

CONTENTS

pg 38

pg 90

pg 109

CONTENTS

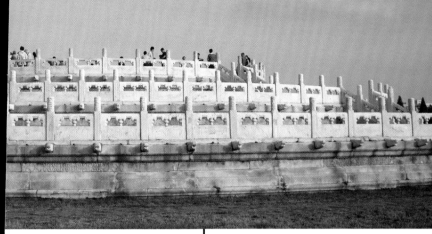

pg 60

pg 134

5

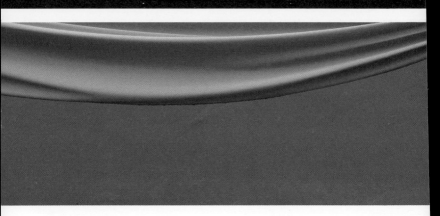

Because time is precious and the travel industry is ever-changing, having accurate, reliable travel information at your fingertips is essential. Mobil Travel Guide has provided invaluable insight to travelers for 50 years, and we are committed to continuing this service into the future.

The Mobil Corporation (known as Exxon Mobil Corporation since a 1999 merger) began producing the Mobil Travel Guide books in 1958 following the introduction of the U.S.-interstate highway system in 1956. The first edition covered only five Southwestern states. Since then, our books have become the premier travel guides in North America, covering all 50 states and Canada.

Since its founding, Mobil Travel Guide has served as an advocate for travelers seeking knowledge about hotels, restaurants and places to visit. Based on an objective process, we make recommendations to our customers that we believe will enhance the quality and value of their travel experiences. Our trusted Mobil One- to Five-Star rating system is the oldest and most respected lodging and restaurant inspection and rating program in North America. Most hoteliers, restaurateurs and industry observers favorably regard the rigor of our inspection program and understand the prestige and benefits that come with receiving a Mobil Star rating.

The Mobil Travel Guide process of rating each establishment includes:

★ Unannouced facility inspections
★ Incognito service evaluations
★ A review of unsolicited comments from the general public
★ Senior management oversight

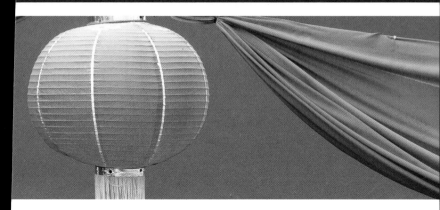

For each property, more than 500 attributes, including cleanliness, physical facilities and employee attitude and courtesy, are measured and evaluated to produce a mathematically derived score, which is then blended with other elements to form an overall score. These scores form the basis that we use to assign our Mobil One- to Five-Star ratings.

This process focuses on guest expectations, guest experience and consistency of service, not just physical facilities and amenities. It's fundamentally a rating system that rewards those properties that continually strive for and achieve excellence each year. The very best properties are consistently raising the bar for those that wish to compete with them.

Only facilities that meet Mobil Travel Guide's standards earn the privilege of being listed in the guide. Deteriorating, poorly managed establishments are deleted. A Mobil Travel Guide listing constitutes a positive quality recommendation. Every listing is an accolade, a recognition of achievement.

We hope that your travels are outstanding and that our books help you get the most out of every trip you take. If any aspect of your accommodation, dining, spa or sightseeing experience motivates you to comment, please contact us at Mobil Travel Guide, 200 W. Madison St., Suite 3950, Chicago, IL 60606, or send an e-mail to info@mobiltravelguide.com. Happy travels.

MOBIL RATED HOTELS

Whether you're looking for the ultimate in luxury or the best bang for your travel buck, we have a hotel recommendation for you. To help you pinpoint properties that meet your needs, Mobil Travel Guide classifies each lodging by type according to the following characteristics.

★★★★★The Mobil Five-Star hotel provides consistently superlative service in an exceptionally distinctive luxury environment, with expanded services. Attention to detail is evident throughout the hotel, resort or inn, from bed linens to staff uniforms.

★★★★The Mobil Four-Star hotel provides a luxury experience with expanded amenities in a distinctive environment. Services may include automatic turndown service, 24-hour room service and valet parking.

★★★⁺The Mobil Three-Star Plus hotel is as luxuriously appointed as a Four-Star hotel, but service is not quite as attentive or reliable as at the Four-Star level. Expect a superb experience in a beautiful setting.

★★★The Mobil Three-Star hotel is well appointed, with a full-service restaurant and expanded amenities, such as a fitness center, golf course, tennis courts, 24-hour room service and optional turndown service.

★★The Mobil Two-Star hotel is considered a clean, comfortable and reliable establishment that has expanded amenities, such as a full-service restaurant on the premises.

★The Mobil One-Star lodging is a limited-service hotel, motel or inn that is considered a clean, comfortable and reliable establishment.

Recommended A Mobil-recommended property is a reliable, standout property new to our guides at press time. Look for a Mobil star-rating for these properties in the future.

For every property, we also provide pricing information. The pricing categories break down as follows:

$ = Up to $150
$$ = $151-$250
$$$ = $251-$350
$$$$ = $351 and up

All prices quoted are accurate at the time of publication, however prices cannot be guaranteed.

RESTAURANTS AND SPAS

Those familiar with Mobil Travel Guides know that we usually rate restaurants and hotel and resort spas along with hotels in each destination. Because service standards vary widely in Beijing compared to North American restaurants and spas, we chose to simply recommend establishments in this city guide. All restaurants and spas in this guide have been visited, taste-tested and experienced by a Mobil Travel Guide writer—you can trust that you'll have a unique, satisfying experience when trying out one of our recommended restaurants or spas.

Because menu prices can fluctuate, we list a pricing category rather than specific prices. The pricing categories are defined as follows, per diner, and assume that you order an appetizer or dessert, an entrée and one drink:

$ = $15 and under
$$ = $16-$35
$$$ = $36-$85
$$$$ = $86 and up

Dining in Beijing can be an incredibly wallet-friendly experience, so you may be surprised to find that a generous-portioned, authentic meal costs well under $15. Prices quoted are accurate at the time of publication, but prices cannot be guaranteed.

BEST OF
BEIJING

A SHORT LIST OF THE TOP EXPERIENCES THIS EXCITING CITY HAS TO OFFER

Grand Hyatt

Gardens at the Shangri-La Hotel

Best Hotels

✳For all-around convenience, great service and superlative rooms, check in at the **Grand Hyatt** or the **Peninsula Beiijing**, locally considered one of the top hotels in town.

✳Beautiful décor; a gracious, accommodating staff; and one of Beijing's best seafood restaurants (Blu Lobster), make the **Shangri-La** a sybaritic escape—just prepare for long commutes to the city center from its remote location.

✳Following a pre-Olympics freshening, the **St. Regis** now has it all—luxurious rooms, top-notch service and a great Chaoyang District location from which to explore the city.

✳Early 20th-century charm and a spectacular location near the Forbidden City make the luxurious **Raffles Hotel** a great choice for those who like both convenience and pampering.

Best Experiences

❋You may have dined on Peking duck before, but nowhere is it more delicious than the city where it originated. In Beijing, perfect roast duck is ordered ahead of a visit, slow roasted and removed from the oven just as you arrive at the restaurant. Purists (and tourists) haunt **Li Qun** or **Da Dong Roast Duck** restaurants for no-frills experiences. Those on expense accounts visit **Made in China** in the **Grand Hyatt** for a more luxe version.

❋A hike along any one of the accessible sections of the **Great Wall** is unforgettable—prepare for steep ascents and descents and plenty of hawkers selling drinks, T-shirts and candy along the way.

❋**Haggling for jade or pearls** (or any kind of knock-off, souvenir or garment, for that matter) at one of Beijing's markets is a sport in itself. Locals advise to offer a price that's less than 50 percent of what you think the item is worth, haggle until it hurts, and be prepared to walk away if you don't reach an agreement on price.

Best Souvenirs

❋There's nothing more au courant than coming home from

Great Wall of China

Beijing with a photograph or artwork from one of the city's many contemporary artists. You can find such a treasure at **798 Art District,** a Soviet-era electronics factory complex that's been turned into a maze of galleries, restaurants and hip coffee houses.

❋China supplies the majority of the world's **cultured freshwater pearls.** Bargaining for a strand (or two or three) is a fun challenge that makes bringing home the spoils of your shopping trip even more worthwhile. Look for pearls in the stalls at the Hongqiao (Pearl) Market near the Temple of Heaven.

Centro

Best Nightlife

✳️See live music at the newly opened **Yugong Yishan,** where international and local rock bands perform for a chic mix of Beijingers and expats.

✳️The sexy, swanky atmosphere at the Philippe Starck–designed **LAN** makes a worldly spot for a cocktail (and the fusion food is delicious, too).

✳️To experience an after-work happy hour like a local, swig an expertly-made martini at the contemporary, streamlined **Centro** in the **Kerry Centre Hotel**, where nightly entertainment includes everything from jazz bands to karaoke.

Best Sights

✳️**The Forbidden City** is impressive, but if you enter at the south side of the museum, you'll leave the most beautiful part of the complex for last: the **Imperial Garden**, a gorgeous maze of pavilions, cypress trees and landscaped pathways. The northeast corner holds the infamous well where Empress Dowager Cixi condemned her son's concubine, Zhen Fei, to death.

✳️Empress Dowager Cixi created the new **Summer Palace**, just miles north of downtown Beijing, on the shores of a beau

Forbidden City

Temple of Heaven

tiful lake and stayed there for almost 20 years, sending her son to rule from the Forbidden City and report back regularly. It's easy to see why she chose to stay—the area is a tranquil retreat of hills, gardens, majestic temples and great views of the lake, and it's usually cooler than the city on hot days.

✳Built in 1420, the **Temple of Heaven** is a sprawling complex of temples, gardens and pavilions frequented today by the city's many retirees, who gather daily to play mahjong or exercise in the park. Tourists love to visit the Echo Wall and test its amazing acoustics or simply marvel at the colorful, majestic Hall of Prayer for Good Harvests, the epicenter of the temple complex.

✳The smell of incense is overwhelming at the **Lama Temple (Yonghegong)**, a Tibetan Buddhist structure on the north side of the city. Real monks watch over the Maitreya Buddha, an 80-foot-tall statue carved from one piece of sandalwood that's listed in *Guinness World Records*. If you're a believer, purchase incense sticks from any of the vendors who line the streets outside the temple and give your offering to the gods.

✳Take a seat at an outdoor café on a warm Beijing day to enjoy the scene at the city's back lakes. The restaurants along **Lotus Lane** stretching to **Houhai Lake** provide seats along the water.

Lama Temple

PHOTO: ROBERT CHURCHILL/iSTOCKPHOTO

Beijing cityscape

ANCIENT CITY,
MODERN TIMES

Beijing's various names throughout history parallel the story of this great city. The city has been called Zhongdu, Ji, Yanjing, Beiping, then Peking, and so on. Beijing has been the capital of China off and on for many dynasties since the first millennium B.C. Today's name means simply "northern capital" and has been the accepted moniker for the past 60 years, since Chairman Mao created the People's Republic of China.

In a country that prides itself on both a long and distinguished past and unparalleled economic growth, it's not surprising that China's modern-day capital is a mesh of ancient history and cutting-edge modernity.

The first recorded dynasty (Xia) dates back some 4,000 years, on the cusp between history and legend. It was ruled, according to lore, by the Yellow Emperor, Huangdi. Zhoulu, to the west of Beijing, is thought to be the first settlement of the area. Here, Huangdi's successor, Yao, is said to have established a capital called Youdu, or "city of calm." Agriculture thrived, and the city's residents traded with the surrounding nomadic tribes.

The Rise and Fall of the Ming and Qing Dynasties

The Ming and Qing Dynasties carried China through some of the most crucial centuries of its early existence. Ruling from 1368 to 1644, the Ming Dynasty rose to power after the collapse of the Mongol-led Yuan Dynasty. The Ming was responsible for improving the military power of China as well as the domestic infrastructure. A navy and standing army of more than one million troops was constructed under Ming rule, allowing China to remain a player in the ever-growing tributary fleet trading system. Ming sovereignty was also responsible for the restoration of the Grand Canal, the building of the Great Wall and the creation of the Forbidden City, a section of Beijing that would later become the capital of the dynasty. As the dynasty grew, so did its opposition and in 1644, the Qing Dynasty captured Beijing, defeated the Ming and ended its near three-century reign. Hailing from Manchuria, the Qing (also known as the Manchu Dynasty) was the last Imperial dynasty of China. From the outset, the dynasty became heavily integrated in Chinese culture, but international pressures and frequent rebellions wore on the Qing, forcing its last emperor, at just five years old, to abdicate his throne.

During the Warring States Period (about 475 to 221 B.C.), the Marquis of the state of Yan annexed the region and established his capital, probably near the White Cloud Temple in present-day Beijing.

In the early third century B.C., the Qin Dynasty took power, and Emperor Qin Shi Huang began to unite the country under a feudal structure. Emperor Qin made Ji the administrative center of a prefecture within his realm. Throughout the next millennium, the city was a key fulcrum in struggles over trade, territory and power. During this period, Emperor Taizong of the Tang Dynasty built the Temple for Compassion for the Loyal where the Temple of the Origin of the Dharma now stands outside the walls of the old city.

At the end of the Tang Dynasty, the Qidans (also known as the Khitans) moved in from the north and made the city the southern capital of the new Liao Dynasty, aptly enough calling it Nanjing or Yanjing, meaning "southern capital." Emperor Taizong of the Liao Dynasty (916–1125) initiated many reconstruction projects, building fortifications as a base from which to conquer China's central plains.

In the early 12th century, the Jurchen or Nuzhen tribe from the northeast conquered the Liao and established the Jin Dynasty. In 1153, Wan Yanliang moved the capital from the present-day Liaoning province to Yanjing and renamed the city Zhongdu, meaning "central capital." From this strategic position, the emperor threatened the Southern Song, whose capital was in present-day Hangzhou. Again, the city saw massive construction, and it reached a population of about 1 million. In 1215, Mongol armies led by Ghengis Khan invaded Zhongdu and made it a provincial capital of his empire. Then in 1271, Kublai Khan founded the Yuan Dynasty and moved the main capital to Zhongdu. He gave the city the Chinese name of Dadu, meaning "great capital," though in Mongol it was known as Khanbalig, "the city of the great Khan." Kublai Khan built numerous imperial palaces and government offices; city walls and moats; and the Tonghui Canal, which connected the capital to the Grand Canal. Significant buildings included the Taimiao (Imperial Ancestral Temple) and Shejitan (Altar of Land and Grain). In addition, streets were laid out in the rational grid pattern, still reflected in the city today, with main streets being 24

Monument in Tiananmen Square

PHOTO: ALAN CRAWFORD/iSTOCKPHOTO

The Forbidden City

The Great Explorer: Marco Polo

As one of the first Westerners to travel the Silk Road to China and visit the mysterious Kublai Khan of the Mongol Empire, Marco Polo gained fame as a worldwide explorer and raconteur of China's exotic cultures. At age 15, Polo, accompanied by his father and uncle, trekked eastward and reached the Great Khan Empire in 1275. Khan liked the youthful Polo and drafted him as a personal confidant. Polo remained in China for 24 years, serving in high-level government positions and inundating himself with the customs of the Far East. Upon return to Venice in 1292 as an escort to a Mongol princess, he joined the army and became imprisoned in Genoa. During his two-year sentence, Marco dictated an account of his travels to a fellow prisoner. *The Travels of Marco Polo* was published shortly thereafter, bringing the story of the Far East to the Western world.

PHOTO: JENNIFER ABRAMSON

paces wide and side streets 12 paces wide. Visitors from far and wide, including Marco Polo, wrote admiringly of the capital city.

Kublai Khan's armies conquered the Southern Song in 1279, uniting China under a central government based in Dadu. In 1368, however, the Yuan Dynasty was overthrown by Ming troops. The founder of the Ming Dynasty, Zhu Yuanzhang, renamed the city Beiping, meaning "northern peace," and made Nanjing, hundreds of miles to the south, his capital. In the 1400s, when Emperor Yongle of the Ming Dynasty fortified the city (with walls that were 12 meters high and 10 meters thick and took 15 years to build) and moved the capital there once more, he named it Beijing, meaning "northern capital."

During this period, Yongle also commissioned a new imperial palace. This palace was called the Forbidden City, because most of the city's population was kept well outside the palace's walls. The Palace was set on the north-south axis of the city, known as Danei, meaning "the great within," and the halls and gates were arranged around this axis. Today it is also known as the Palace Museum. The sprawl-

ing, majestic Temple of Heaven was also built during the 1420s as a place for royal worship.

In 1644, the Manchus took over Beijing and established the Qing Dynasty. Their legacy is the gardens and palaces they built throughout the city. The most famous of these is the Old Summer Palace, or Yuanmingyuan, which took about 150 years to complete and covered more than 864 acres. During the Second Opium War in the 1860s, the British-French Allied Forces burned Yuanmingyuan and plundered the imperial library there.

By the early 20th century, the Qing Dynasty had weakened and become corrupt. The Empress Dowager Cixi, as politically ruthless as she was astute and ultimately as corrupt, ruled for half a century, first through her son and then through her nephew. She spent lavishly on building a new Summer Palace, where she lived for years, sending the nominal emperor to the Forbidden City to carry out her orders. She died in 1908, and in 1911, revolutionaries overthrew the rule of 5-year-old Emperor Puyi (often called the "last emperor," see box, page 22).

The Last Emperor of the Qing Dynasty

Often acknowledged as the last Emperor of China, Puyi assumed the throne in 1908, when he was just two years old. Puyi's childhood innocence vanished virtually overnight as he was swept away to the Forbidden City and transformed to the God-like stature of an emperor. His ascension came during a difficult period for the Qing Dynasty with foreign powers pressing for domination, and political turmoil shadowed his short reign. In 1911 with the advice of his father as regent, Puyi renounced his throne and became a non-ruling emperor until 1924. He rose again to power in 1934 as the Kangde Emperor of Manchukuo, but his initial abdication remained a symbol of the end of one of China's longest, most infamous eras.

Beijing remained the capital with Yuan Shikai as president. But in 1915, he tried to re-establish an imperial government and make himself emperor. Turmoil followed. Yuan Shikai died (of natural causes) within a year. The Japanese invaded and occupied the city from 1937 until the end of World War II; then the stage was set for historic change. On October 1, 1949, Mao Zedong declared from Tiananmen Square that China would be renamed the People's Republic of China. The city once again became the capital of the country and was renamed Beijing.

During Mao's Cultural Revolution of the 1960s, much of the culture and history of Beijing was destroyed in the name of progress. An unknown number of priceless ancient relics all over the country, including Beijing, were lost. Most of the city's ancient walls were

torn down to make way for the modern ring roads, and even the Forbidden City was threatened with destruction. Traditional arts, like Beijing opera, were banned, with many performers going into "retirement." Many returned at the end of the Cultural Revolution to revive the art, which thrives today.

After Mao's death in 1976, Deng Xiaoping came to power, and his economic reforms helped to urbanize and modernize Beijing quickly. With economic growth came massive urban sprawl, which replaced the surrounding farmland with factories.

Some believed the reforms hadn't gone in the right direction politically. In the late 1970s, a construction wall in Beijing became the "Democracy Wall" on which people began pasting posters criticizing the government. Activists were swiftly arrested and punished for their resistance. In 1989, protesters went on a hunger strike in Tiananmen Square. The People's Liberation Army famously rolled into Tiananmen Square with tanks and killed hundreds, perhaps thousands, of protesters on June 4. Protest leaders were jailed and related officials were removed.

Although political reform was quashed, economic reform has continued, leading to unprecedented economic growth and the capacity to host an Olympic games in Beijing. Beijing now has more than 17 districts and spans more than 6,900 square feet. The surrounding counties have been incorporated into the city as part of the Beijing municipality. Despite the new developments and modern architecture, particularly the construction and development surrounding the Olympic Games, efforts have been made to preserve the city's original layout. Many things remain the same, like the city's chessboard-like structure; this blend of new and old can be seen everywhere.

Urban areas are expanding, as are the problems that come with them, like increased smog, pollution, traffic and loss of historic neighborhoods. However, parts of traditional Beijing, like Liulichang Culture Street, have been restored. As the capital of one of the world's largest countries and most powerful economies, this city is well on its way to live up to its storied past.

BEIJING
SNAPSHOT

Beijing essentials

Beijing is a fascinating, sprawling, forward-marching megalopolis of 17 million people. Before you arrive or explore Beijing, consider the following.

Four wheels are better than two

Ask anyone who visited Beijing a decade ago, and they'll tell you about the incredible number of people riding bicycles throughout the city. With the opening of China to the West and access to affordable cars, bikes have largely been abandoned for automobiles. This has fueled the tangle of traffic that enmeshes the city around the clock. As for driving in Beijing, the rule is almost that there are no rules, so leave the driving to the pros (taxis) and enjoy the view.

Breathing easy

Beijing's pollution is as much a favorite topic of locals (who love to complain about it) as it is with vis-itors who have never experienced smog like this. Many of Beijing's factories burn coal and other fuels that contribute to the pollution (think Victorian London). On the worst days, a thick haze hangs over the city and stings eyes and lungs. Some hopeful locals don medical masks to keep out the pollutants. Attempts by the government to reduce smog artificially by firing rain-causing chemicals into the sky (bizarre, but true) may or may not help, but they are at least an attempt at improvement.

Economies of scale

Beijing is huge. And most local maps are deceiving in scale—what looks like a short walk could be closer to a three-mile trek. A walk from some Dongcheng hotels to the Forbidden City, which on a map appears just a few blocks, could take as long as 30 minutes. Add to the mix the incredible volume of traffic at all hours of the day, and you've got

PHOTO: COURTESY LEONARDO.COM

The Forbidden City

Beijing at night

a city that can be tough to get around. When going anywhere— for dinner reservations, a theater performance or to meet a friend—plan at least 30 minutes more than you think you will need and prepare to sit in traffic.

Gulp—is the water safe?

Visitors are discouraged from drinking the tap water in Beijing, but accidental or minimal exposure (like when you're brushing your teeth) won't usually cause any problems. Unlike the biological risks associated with drinking water in some other developing nations, the issue here is the presence of various metals, residues and minerals picked up from aging pipes.

Chinarazzi

When visiting tourist destinations, you will be among many domestic tourists who are experiencing their first trip to an international city. Many come from outlying or rural areas, and they may be seeing a non-Chinese person for the first time. Don't be surprised to see someone pointing a camera at you, especially if you have young children with you. Expect an often overwhelming number of requests for photos and people curiously touching your child's hair (especially if it's blond or red). If all the attention gets out of control, you can simply say, "Bu yao (boo yow)." This is the same thing you would say in the markets to overly aggressive vendors, and it means "I don't want it or need it." The polite way to ask people to put their cameras away is "Qing bu yao jiao (ching boo yao jow)," which means "Please do not take."

Beijing or Beverly Hills

When driving around Beijing, you will see quite a few imported, premium-brand cars like Audi, BMW, Porsche and Mercedes, something that's fairly new to the capital city. Some are being manufactured in China, but with duty (on imported parts) and luxury taxes, these vehicles sometimes cost three times as much as in other places. A Volkswagen Touareg, which costs approximately $45,000 in the United States, will set a local back $120,000. A 7-Series BMW costs about $250,000 (at least twice as much as in the United States). Many factors affect these prices, but either way, it's evident that there is lot of new money in China. A flashy ride is just one of the many new ways Beijingers are expressing their wealth—try to keep count of the number of Gucci stores you see during your visit.

Dress code

Regardless of your style, you should appreciate the fact that Beijing is a city that isn't afraid to take design risks with fashion and architecture. The range of men's and women's clothing varies from simple, conservative elegance to an enigmatic mix of patterns. The same is true with the architecture. Bold designs are making Beijing an enjoyable place to sightsee while driving around.

One of the most entertaining aspects of design in Beijing comes from the restroom facilities of upscale restaurants, nightclubs and hotel bars, where you'll see ultra-contemporary spaces that have received as much thoughtful design and careful execution as the rest of the establishment. That said, casual fashion rules here, and anything goes for a night out.

Time for a change

Beijing has experienced painful economic and social growth with tremendous pressure to be more "culturally evolved" according to Western standards. People who return to China after a brief absence always comment on how much everything has changed. With (or despite) this pace of change, people are basking in the glow of the spotlight thanks to the 2008 Olympics. The country's leaders don't see the concept of "global domination" in the same way that Western nations have throughout history. China wants to gain power peacefully through economic growth, and foreign policy focuses on commercial trade, not militaristic alliance or action. As such, the average Chinese person is usually neutral towards most foreign nationalities and happy to share their city with the foreigners flocking to it.

Emperor's Temple at
the Summer Palace

WHAT TO SEE

CAPITAL **IDEA**

A sprawling, massive city ringed by a series of five different ring roads, Beijing got its start as a small northern outpost and grew to become the Chinese capital off and on throughout its history. The original city's walls were pulled down during the Cultural Revolution, but there are still plenty of buildings surviving to remind visitors of the city's importance as a seat of government for thousands of years. With three World Heritage sites (the Forbidden City, the Summer Palace and the Temple of Heaven), Buddhist temples and gorgeous Ming dynasty courtyards, there are reminders of Beijing's past everywhere, even as the city is changing dramatically for the future.

Architecture buffs will be amazed by the volume of new, futuristic buildings, from the National Center for the Performing Arts to the wildly unique CCTV headquarters. Since most sights are outdoors, a visit to Beijing is best in warmer months, even if that means sharing your experience with throngs of crowds.

Dongcheng

This neighborhood is the historic heart of the city and contains many of Beijing's most important sites, including the Forbidden City, Tiananmen Square and the Lama Temple. You'll also find plenty of intimate, ancient hutongs, some of which now have boutique hotels or restaurants (but still deliver plenty of authenticity and vibrancy). Wangfujing is Beijing's busy pedestrian-only shopping street, with plenty of international brands alongside local shops.

Forbidden City

Zijin Cheng, 010-6513-2255; www.dpm.org.cn; Daily: 8:30 a.m.-5:30 p.m and 8:30 a.m.-4:30 p.m, winter.

The imperial palace for emperors of the Ming and Qing dynasties is a museum in and of itself. Building began in 1406 under Ming emperor Yongle, and the Forbidden City's (so-called because commoners were forbidden to enter the royal palace) almost 9,000 rooms make it the largest in the world. This World Heritage site is located inside the original city of Beijing's walls at its center and is

The Forbidden City

Beijing in One Day

Begin early at **Tiananmen Square** and take in the sights of both Chairman Mao's portrait on the **Gate of Heavenly Peace** and his body in repose at **Chairman Mao's** mausoleum. Make your way to the **Forbidden City** and spend the better part of an afternoon exploring its many (almost 9,000 in total) buildings. If time permits, squeeze in a visit (by subway) to the **Temple of Heaven,** before returning to **Wangfujing** for some retail therapy. Finish your day with afternoon tea at the historic **Raffles Hotel** or roast duck at **Quanjude Roast Duck Restaurant** or **Made in China** at the **Grand Hyatt**.

Beijing in Three Days

Start your second day with a pilgrimage to the new and old **Summer Palaces**. Or opt for a half-day visit to the **Great Wall** at Badaling or Mutianyu. Make plans to see an opera or acrobatic performance at one of the city's many theaters, and then head to **Sanlitun Bar Street** or one of the outdoor cafés at **Beihai Park.**

Spend another day shopping the wares at the **Silk Market** or browsing for contemporary art at **798 Art District.** Make time for a stop at the fragrant **Lama Temple** to see the world's largest Buddha carved from a single piece of wood. End the night with dinner at a courtyard restaurant such as **Red Capital Club**, or by catching one of Beijing's hottest local bands at music club **D-22**.

surrounded by moat. Though vast, it is not difficult to walk around the entire place in half a day, especially since many buildings are closed to the public. Some portions are also closed due to construction or are covered in scaffolding—a massive restoration that began in 2005 is still in progress. It's hard to believe that this sprawling, majestic complex was almost lost during the fervor of the Cultural Revolution, when symbols of the old Chinese dynasties were destroyed in favor of progress for the new People's Republic. The Forbidden City covers more than 860,000 square yards and a distance of 3,150 feet from north to south and 2,470 feet from east to west. A moat 170 feet wide, which freezes over in winter, sur-

The Olympic Countdown at
Tiananmen Square

rounded the palace as did stone walls 32 feet high. The Inner Courtyard was the domain of the emperors and their many servants while the Outer Courtyard hosted official ceremonies.

During its 491-year tenure as an imperial palace, 24 different emperors ruled from the Forbidden City, from Zhu Di, the third Ming emperor, to Puyi, the last Qing emperor. Inside the 32-foot-high walls are dozens of red-lacquered pavilions, walkways, courtyards and pagodas, all arranged and decorated with symbolic meaning. In its heyday, the imperial palace was filled with thousands of servants, concubines, eunuchs, laborers and officials, all living under the direction of the emperor.

Most visitors enter through the Gate of Heavenly Peace, the historic location of Chairman Mao's address to the people on the founding of the People's Republic of China. Mao's portrait still hangs above the entrance to the gate and provides one of Beijing's most iconic photo ops. Once inside the south gates, buy an all-inclusive ticket and spring for the handy automated audio tour (ignoring the ubiquitous offers for English-language guides). A Starbucks outlet famously sprung up near this entrance in 2000, but public outcry over the stark commercialism of this move in such a sacred place led to its removal by 2007. The buildings, their colors and their arrangement within the palace walls all contain symbolism.

Each building is topped with a yellow-tiled roof (symbolizing the royal residence) and a number of dragon or phoenix figures placed to protect against fire. Most of the buildings in the Forbidden City were made of wood with stone courtyards and steps. Fire was a major concern (with some entire halls burned throughout the history of the palace) so large copper water cauldrons were positioned around each building that can still be seen today. Structures that housed important paper documents or treasures were denoted with black-tiled roofs (black being the symbolic color of water).

The largest building in the complex is the Hall of Supreme Harmony, an outer courtyard throne building from which emperors conducted official business. A carved stone ramp decorated with dragons leads to the hall, and was available only for the emperor's use. In the inner courtyard lie three buildings, the Palace of Heavenly Purity, the Hall of Union and the Palace of Earthly Tranquility. These made up the royal bedrooms and living spaces. The Hall of Mental Cultivation served as the Empress Cixi Dowager and the last emperor Puyi's living quarters. At the north end of the palace is the Imperial Flower Garden, a peaceful, landscaped space of pavilions and pagodas that provided the royals with a taste of nature within the Forbidden City's walls. The northeast corner of the garden contains the Well of the Concubine Zhen, rumored to be the spot where the Empress Dowager Cixi disposed of the concubine Zhen Fei, her son Guangxu's favorite. The Gate of the Divine Warrior is the northern exit to the complex, and Jingshan (or Coal Hill) across the street provides a panoramic view of the palace.

Tiananmen Square

This sprawling, concrete plaza is the world's largest public square. Since imperial days, Tiananmen has functioned as a gathering spot for public functions. For a seemingly innocuous stretch of space, some of Beijing's most important events have taken place here.

In 1919, protestors gathered on May 4th to demand government reforms, and on October 1, 1949 Chairman Mao proclaimed the People's Republic of China from the square's northern side. For most Westerners, the square is in-

extricably linked with the events of 1989, when thousands of students and pro-democracy protestors gathered in the square and were quickly put down by Chinese military troops on foot and in tanks.

The square as it stands today took shape in the late 1950s when Chairman Mao ordered the area quadrupled in size and covered in concrete so that it could hold as many as a million people. The Monument to the People's Heroes, a stone obelisk, was added to the middle of the square to honor those who fell in the revolution, from the Opium Wars to the founding of the People's Republic. The southern end of the square holds Chairman Mao's mausoleum, while the east and west sides are bordered by the massive National Museum of China (closed at press time for renovations) and the Great Hall of the People, the meeting space for the Chinese parliament. Two majestic gates border the square, with the Gate of Heavenly Peace serving as the entrance to the Forbidden City, and Qiamen Gate a reminder of what's left of the ancient city's walls. The Gate of Heavenly Peace, or Tiananmen Gate, stands on the location of a wood bridge constructed in 1417 that was damaged by fire and rebuilt in stone in the 1460s. Emperors would leave

Soldiers in Tiananmen Square

Main gate at Tiananmen Square adorned with a photo of Chairman Mao

the Forbidden City en route to the Temple of Heaven via this gate, making their first offerings here or pausing to deliver official messages to the people residing outside the palace walls. Mao Zedong chose the spot as a symbolically imperial place to declare the founding of a new republic, and it is now the only building in Beijing to publicly display Mao's portrait.

Qianmen (or Front Gate) dates to 1421 and includes Jianlou (Arrow Tower) and the wooden gate Zhengyangmen, both of which can be toured. Each day at sunset, the military guard goes through the ceremony of lowering the Chinese flag, so that when it's raised again the next day the sun symbolically rises anew on China. It's a powerful and fascinating ritual that makes for a memorable experience, morning or night.

Zedong Mao Memorial Hall
Tiananmen Square; Tuesday-Sunday: 8:30 a.m.-11:30 a.m; Tuesday-Thursday: 2 p.m.-4 p.m.
Line up with the throngs of Chinese visitors in Tiananmen Square for a chance to view the mummified body of the founder of the People's Republic of China lying in repose. Mao Zedong died in September 1976 and was placed in the mausoleum constructed in

his honor soon after on the site of the old Zhonghua Gate. Visitors are not allowed to bring bags or cameras into the solemn space, so plan accordingly. The shops placed strategically near the exit to the mausoleum contain plenty of Mao-era kitsch, including lighters, key rings and other knickknacks.

Wangfujing
This stretch of commercialism is Beijing's most popular shopping street. The pedestrian-only street is a favorite weekend gathering spot of city dwellers who come here to browse through the Niketowns and Adidas shops, have tea at the glass-enclosed tea shops or sample any of the street food on offer, including grilled sweet potatoes or ears of corn. The thoroughfare was once called Morrison Street by the westerners who lived nearby in the Foreign Legations Quarter after an Australian newspaper correspondent who lived on the street. Nearby is the Donganmen Night Market where vendors hawk everything from skewered crickets to lamb satay once the sun sets.

Foreign Legation Quarter
Tucked away to the east of Tiananmen Square lies a Colonial-style neighborhood that housed foreign delegates, businesses and officials until the 1950s and the

Temple of Heaven

launch of the People's Republic of China. Here you'll find European-style buildings now cleverly appropriated for new functions, from the former First National City Bank of New York (now the Beijing Police Museum) to the former French post office, now the Jingyuan Sichaun Restaurant. Other buildings include the former French, British, Austro-Hungarian and Belgian legations, the Banque de l'Indochine and the site of the former Grand Hotel des Wagon-Lits, once the most stylish hotel in town. The Beijing City Planning Museum (20 Qianmen Dongdajie) has dis-

plays on the city's structures covering 3,000 years of history.

Lama Temple

Yonghegong Daijie; Daily
8:00 a.m.-4:30 p.m.
You can smell the Lama Temple, or Yonghe Gong, before you actually enter it thanks to the dozens of incense stands lining the streets outside the temple walls. This is the holiest Tibetan temple in the city, and the former home of Count Yin Zhen, who became Emperor Yongzheng and moved to the Forbidden City in 1723. The space was transformed into a monas-

PHOTO: KINABALOO.COM

tery for monks from Tibet and Mongolia in 1744. A series of six halls houses various shrines to Buddha, culminating in the impressive Wanfu Pavilion and its Maitreya Buddha, a 60-foot-tall specimen said to be carved from a single piece of sandalwood.

Chongwen and Xuanwu

These neighborhoods, located south of Tiananmen Square, are some of the most densely populated. You'll find the Temple of Heaven and the Pearl Market in Chongwen, as well as several old hutongs (one of which contains the famed Li Qun Duck Restaurant). Xuanwu is home to the city's Muslim population; the Niujie Mosque and busy Ox Street make for a worthwhile excursion

Temple of Heaven
Yongdingmen Dajie; Daily 8:00 a.m.-4:30 p.m.
It should be no surprise that the impressive red-washed, intricate temples that make up this Taoist worship complex were built during the same period and under the same direction of the same emperor as those of the Forbidden City. From 1406 to 1420 this magnificent complex of parks, temples and pavilions were constructed

Summer Palace

as a place for emperors to pray for ample harvests, rain or other favors for the people from the gods. Today, it's one of the most popular city parks, filled daily with locals who come to exercise, socialize and relax and tourists who come to marvel at the red-hued structures. Recently, the Temple underwent a massive restoration. Three main buildings make up the temple complex, which include the Hall of Prayer for Good Harvests, the Imperial Vault of Heaven, and the Earthly Mount. All of the structures of the temple were built in accordance with symbolic beliefs. Earth is represented by a circle, while heaven takes the shape of a square.

Though the Temple of Heaven was once the official praying ground for past emperors, it's more than just a serious, solemn place. Its famous Echo Wall keeps tourists busy as two people stand on opposite ends of the wall and whisper—and are able to hear each other. The largest complex of temples in China, the Temple of Heaven also houses the earthly mount, a circular mound of three levels from which the emperor would offer sacrifices and prayers. The color blue which is used to symbolize the color of the sky and therefore heaven, unifies the buildings.

Niujie (Ox Street) Mosque
Niu Jie; Daily 8 a.m.-sunset
Beijing's southern section was home to its Muslim population, and it has the city's oldest and biggest mosque. Built during the Northern Song Dynasty more than 1,000 years ago, the mosque remains a popular spot for worship and includes a Chinese-style prayer hall and courtyard garden.

Haidian
Once quiet countryside, this neighborhood northwest of the third ring road is the city's university area, with both Peking University and Tsinghua University (the nation's top technology school) located here. There are also fascinating historic sights, including the new and old Summer Palaces, the Beijing Zoo and Beijing Botanical Garden.

Summer Palace
Yiheyuan Lu; Daily 6:30 a.m.-4:30 p.m.
One of Beijing's most beautiful spaces is the Summer Palace, the one-time home of the extravagant Empress Dowager Cixi. The "new" Summer Palace, also called Yiheyuan, or garden of cultivated harmony, had been a favorite royal garden for decades which was transformed into the complex seen today after the ransacking of the old Summer

Beijing

PHOTO: KINABALOO.COM

Beihai Park

Palace. Cixi directed the building of the temples, pavilions, gardens and lake at her retreat, and was so pleased with the result she stayed at the Summer Palace on and off until her death in 1908, abandoning the Forbidden City. When you enter this park, located in northern Beijing near Peking University, you'll find people singing in the entry corridor, playing traditional Chinese instruments or doing tai chi in the grassy area behind the corridor and beneath the picturesque willow trees. These trees provide some much needed shade and coolness from the muggy Beijing heat of summer, as does water, which makes up three-fourths of the premises. With the size of the place, a map is extremely helpful to avoid getting lost.

A fan of Beijing opera, Cixi had an open-air stage constructed in the Garden of Virtue and Harmony, which is now a theater museum displaying costumes, props and other curios. Colorful, cacophonous operas are performed for visitors to the Summer Palace on a regular basis at the open-air theater. Other notable sights on the palace grounds include the Long Corridor, a 796-yard long painted gallery that leads from the entrance to the park to the artificially created

Longevity Hill. A Ming-era temple once stood on the spot which now holds the Temple of Gratitude for a Long Life, built by Emperor Qianlong in honor of his mother Cixi's 60th birthday. The original was destroyed in 1860 and rebuilt in 1892. At the top of the hill is the Pagoda of Buddhist Fragrance, the highest point in the park. Along the shores of the palace's Kunming Lake you'll find the Marble Boat, which Cixi built with money intended for the Chinese navy, an act that many believe led to the Chinese defeat at the hands of the Japanese in 1895. The Seventeen Arches Bridge crosses the lake in an attractive, gentle arc.

Old Summer Palace
Qinghuan Xi Lu; Daily 8 a.m.-5:30 p.m.; summer 7 a.m.-7 p.m.
Ransacked and burned by British and French forces during the Second Opium War, this site was once a retreat for Qing dynasty rulers in warm summer months. The area, also called Yuanmingyuan, which translates to Garden of Perfect Clarity, is a less crowded but just as beautiful alternative to the nearby Summer Palace. Ruins of the old palace, which was built between 1747 and 1759 under the direction of European architects, include stone columns and frescoes that dot the landscape, which is

Panda at Beijing Zoo

crisscrossed by paths and lakes. Emperor Qianlong, who ruled from 1736 through 1795, was a fan of European style and filled the palace with European fountains, furniture, food and music. By the middle of the 1800s, however, China was at war with European imperialists who wanted to open Asian markets for trade. When China, under the rule of Emperor Xianfeng, tried to eject European merchants, British-led forces invaded and ransacked and burned Yuanmingyuan. The soldiers carried out whatever they could find in the palace, with some of the treasures making their way to Western museums and auctions. All of the authentic wooden Chinese buildings burned to the ground, and only some of the stone European-style structures were left standing. Much debate has taken place over whether the palace should be restored, with some arguing that to rebuild would be to triumph over the humiliation of imperialist defeat, and others saying that to reconstruct would destroy the sacred nature of the ruins. Until a decision is made, the palace remains a peaceful spot for escaping the city year-round.

Beijing Zoo
Xizhimenwai Dajie; Daily 7:30 a.m.-6 p.m.
If seeing pandas in their native habitat is on your list of things to do in China, make a stop at Beijing's zoo. Though most of the

PHOTO: KINABALOO.COM

Beijing Botanic Gardens

other animals in the zoo live in drab concrete abodes, recent attempts to convert the space to a more natural environment has improved the look and feel of the place. The area on which today's zoo stands has been a park area since the Ming dynasty. In 1906, under Emperor Guangxu, the area was transformed into a zoo and an agricultural farm, and in 1908 it opened to the public. Years of neglect led to a dwindling population of only 12 monkeys, two parrots and an emu by the time of the launch of the People's Republic. The space was renamed the Beijing Zoo and opened again to the public in 1950. Today's zoo has more than 7,000 animals from 600 different species, including bears, elephants, lions and tigers and of course, the zoo's star Giant Pandas.

Beijing Botanic Gardens
Daily 7 a.m.-5 p.m.
A beautifully landscaped park draped across the rolling acres of the Western Hills, the Botanic Garden is best known for the Sleeping Buddha Temple. A Tang dynasty structure, the building contains a mammoth reclining Buddha. Particularly popular on weekends, the garden is a favorite local retreat from the city's smog and heat.

Fragrant Hills Park
Daily 8 a.m.-6 p.m.
In the northwestern suburbs beyond the Summer Palaces is this park, established during the Jin

dynasty and expanded in the Ming dynasty. It opened to the public in the 1950s. Many of the buildings were destroyed during the Second Opium War, but visitors can still see sights such as the Glazed Tile Pagoda, a building hung with bells that chime in the breeze, and several other temples or pavilions. Beijingers love to visit the park on weekends, particularly in autumn when the sycamore and maple trees turn shades of gold and red.

Chaoyang

The most commercial and newest section of the city is also the location of Beijing's trendiest places to live, eat, work and play. Most of the new, luxury hotels have been built here, as has the newly burgeoning Central Business District. Top shopping malls filled with international brands are springing up throughout the district, and new restaurants with an eye to design as much as to cuisine are boosting the city's culinary scene. Here you'll find Sanlitun Bar Street, a district loaded with lively bars and clubs, and the embassy district and nearby Lido area, where foreigners tend to congregate.

Sanlitun Bar Street

Once one of the seedier nightlife areas of the city, this area has recently been transformed. Vast sections of this neighborhood have been torn down and rebuilt ahead of the Olympics. Many of the bars are still blatantly touristy, but you can find gems (and new ventures open every day) along the main street, Sanlitun Lu.

Ritan Park

Daily 6 a.m.-9 p.m.
Dating to the 1500s, this peaceful city park features lovely landscaping and is centered around an altar that was used for sacrificial offerings to the sun. Today it's more popular with local office workers looking for a quiet alfresco spot for lunch.

Xicheng

Beijing's western section is the sight of a massive new building project centered on the new Financial Street area, where steel and glass towers have sprouted seemingly overnight. Though there are several new international hotels in the neighborhood, the area (particularly after dark) can seem somewhat deserted. Nearby though, is the lovely Beihai Park and Houhai Lake, both of which are great spots to commune with nature or savor a drink at an outdoor café.

Prince Gong's Palace

17 Qianhai Xijie, Daily 8 a.m.-4 p.m.
Opulent traditional opera performances are held in the Qing

dynasty Grand Opera House located on the grounds of this former imperial residence. The buildings and landscaped gardens are thought to have inspired the novel *Dream of the Red Mansions.* Come for a pre-opera stroll in the gardens and stay for an authentic theater experience.

Bell and Drum Towers
Diamen Dajie, Daily, 9 a.m.-4:30 p.m.
Located near Houhai Lake, these towers date to the days of Kublai Khan. The current bell tower was built in 1747 after the original was destroyed by fire. A bronze bell inside the tower was used to wake the city each day at 7 a.m. The structure was so solid it withstood a massive earthquake in 1976 without significant damage. The drum tower once held 24 drums (one survives) which were struck each night at 7 p.m. to signal the end of the day and closing of the city gates. The drums were struck every two hours throughout the night until 5 a.m.

Beihai Park
This city park offers ice skating in winter and a bucolic spot in summer for boating or sampling one of the many restaurants that surround the park's lake. Originally used as an imperial garden and part of the Forbidden City, the park's most recognizable landmark is the White Dagoba, an onion-shaped Tibetan-style tower that provides great views of the Forbidden City.

NATION **BUILDING**

One benefit of the Chinese love of everything new is the embrace of forward-thinking design. As Beijing has modernized, especially on the heels of the Olympic Games, the city's planners have given the green light to some of the most advanced architecture in the world. With no cultural conservatism or historic preservation to hold them back, the city's builders have transformed the skyline into something futuristic and fresh. Here's a look at the some of the top new structures.

Olympic Stadium

Beijing National Stadium (Olympic stadium)

Beijing Olympic Park

When Beijing was awarded the Olympics in 2001, it was seen as a strategic opportunity for the nation to show the world how progressive it is. As such, the new National Stadium needed to be an impressive structure of architectural genius. Perched not far from the ruins of the ancient city wall, the new stadium (dubbed "the bird's nest" by locals) was designed by Swiss firm Herzog & de Meuron, who designed London's Tate Modern Museum. The 80,000-seat stadium is enclosed by a lattice structure of 45,000 tons of steel and glass.

National Aquatics Centre

Beijing Olympic Park

Designed to resemble a shimmering, fluid block of water, this natatorium, constructed expressly for the 2008 games, was designed by Australian firm PTW, which worked previously on venues for the Sydney Olympics. The 17,000-seat structure's exterior is designed to resemble bubbles and is a sight to be seen.

CCTV Headquarters

East Third Ring Middle Road

Rising over the newly buzzing Central Business District is a contemporary glass and steel tower designed by star

PHOTO: MICHAEL BONACCI

Dutch architect Rem Koolhaas and his German protégé Ole Scheeren. The CCTV building, the new home for the Chinese Central Television network, is a feat of modern engineering which features two towers rising to support a cantilevered floor connecting the two in a loop hanging high above the ground below. The complex is one of the most prestigious to be built in the crush of pre-Olympic construction, and will be home to another tower housing the new Mandarin Oriental hotel and plenty of restaurants to feed the hungry office workers in the tower above.

Beijing Capital International Airport Terminal 3

To process all the anticipated Olympic passengers, the Chinese fast-tracked the construction of a new terminal at Capital Airport which opened in spring 2008. The structure, designed by British architect Norman Foster, who also dreamed up Hong Kong's acclaimed airport, is the world's fastest to be built (it was completed in four years). With a design that marries ancient symbols (there's a red roof shaped like a dragon) with modern ideas (expect fully wired capabilities) the terminal is set to be one of the most up-to-date in the world in terms of security.

A Beijing park

Fun in Long Tan Park

Artifacts at the PanJai Yuan Antique Market

PHOTO: KINABALOO

A park near the Beijing Zoo

BEIJING

The Regent Beijing

HOTELS

GRAND **HOTELS**

IN BEIJING, IT'S OUT WITH THE OLD, IN WITH THE NEW

The incredible crush of building construction in 2008 has resulted in scores of new hotels opening their doors to guests seemingly overnight. (More than a dozen International-brand hotels opened in Beijing in 2008 alone.) The sheer volume of new rooms is in stark contrast to the past, when the city was essentially closed to foreign investment and most hotels were stark, government-supported affairs. Travelers to Beijing can now find everything from efficient new budget hotels to extreme luxury presented by familiar global brands.

Twenty-four-hour traffic jams mean being close to public transportation is key to getting around; where to stay is often dictated not only by your budget but by how much time you're willing to put in to getting from point to point.

To be close to the Forbidden City and Tiananmen Square, stay in the Dongcheng district. On the other hand, because of its location on several subway lines, the Chaoyang district's hotels make it easy to navigate the city (and access some of the best shopping and restaurants). Those conducting business in the newly constructed Financial Street area often stay in the brand-new hotels in that neighborhood (though keep in mind that there are few restaurants or services in Xicheng, and the area is something of a ghost town after dark). The hotels located around the Embassy Area are near enough to the popular Sanlitun Bar Street to deliver great clubs and restaurants. And the Lido area is located in a neighborhood populated with expats. If you're in town for a short time and want to be closer to the airport, this neighborhood is a good bet.

The Peninsula Beijing

For a splurge at any hotel, upgrade when possible to a Club Level floor, which often includes free Internet access, all-day snacks, breakfast and concierge services.

If you travel with Mobil often, you know that our star ratings are the result of several rounds of testing more than 550 standards with a value placed on superb service. Because we found English skills to still be limited at many top hotels and service spottier than usual compared to other Asian cities, we've created a new category of 3+ star-rated hotels. These are outstanding hotels with superb facilities that still have just a bit of work to do to get their service up to speed. Why does this matter? When you're paying top dollar for a good night's rest, the hotel staff should do the work for you, from recommending the best restaurant in town (and following through with a taxi driver who knows how to deliver you to the correct address) to assisting with more complicated issues (from helping you find a pharmacy when you're feeling under the weather to assisting in purchasing a swimsuit so you can enjoy the fitness center's sparkling new pool).

Dongcheng District
★★Beijing Hotel
33 Dongchangan Dajie, Dongcheng District, 010-6513-7766; www.chinabeijinghotel. com.cn/en/main.asp
Though frills are few at this large hotel, its location near Tiananmen Square can't be beat—the hotel is adjacent to the more upscale Raffles Beijing and Grand Hotel Beijing. Expect classic décor with an Asian twist, from the fabrics in the rooms to the Chinese-inspired contemporary furnishings. The property includes a number of dining establishments, from a simple café to a Japanese eatery offering sushi, as well as a steakhouse, a distinctive Cantonese restaurant featuring dried fish, and a restaurant offering a range of regional Chinese cuisines. *1,000 rooms. 6 restaurants, bar. Pool. Business center. $*

★★Crowne Plaza Beijing
48 Wangfujing Dajie, Dongcheng District, 010-5911-9999, 877-227-6963 (U.S.); www. ichotelsgroup.com
This recently renovated, centrally located hotel offers one of Beijing's best values. Rooms are smart and modern with duvet-topped beds, flat-screen TVs, and soothing, neutral tones. The

Kempinski Hotel pool

hotel features an updated fitness center and indoor pool. The lobby-level Champagne Bar is a popular city hangout thanks to its live DJs and lounge atmosphere. *360 rooms. 2 restaurants, 2 bars. Airport transportation available. Pool. Fitness center. Business center. $*

★★★Grand Hotel Beijing

35 Dongchangan Dajie, Dongcheng District, 010-6513-7788; www.grandhotelbeijing.com
Those wanting quick access to the Forbidden City and Tiananmen Square check into this upscale hotel, which has plenty of Asian flair from the décor of the sprawling multilevel lobby to the tasteful, classic rooms. Besides a large indoor pool, this hotel offers a fitness center, sauna and weekly exercise classes. The onsite restaurants, Old Pekin and Ming Yuan, serve a range of Chinese cuisine from classic to contemporary. The Fountain Bar is a lively spot for late-night cocktails. *217 rooms. 4 restaurants, bar. Pool. Fitness center. Business center. $$$*

★★★★Grand Hyatt

1 Dongchangan Dajie, Dongcheng District, 010-8518-1234,

COURTYARD **CHARM**

MUCH HAS BEEN made of the steady demolition of Beijing's traditional alleyway residences, or hutongs. These neighborhoods of tiny streets lined with traditional courtyard houses date back to the Qing dynasty, and advocates say they are the last peek into an ancient city that is modernizing faster than anyone can comprehend. Opponents say that they are crumbling, sometimes unsanitary slums. (Some houses still do not have plumbing; their residents use the many public toilets that dot the alleyways). Enterprising hoteliers (including some foreigners) have bought and restored courtyard buildings in the hutongs and opened unique, sometimes gorgeous hostelries. Staying in one of these boutique hotels is an experience unlike any other: though the courtyards are in the middle of the bustling, overcrowded city, there's a unique sense of peace and quiet inside the hutongs. The experience can be chilly in winter (Beijing's notoriously dry, cold winters make the ancient buildings and their sometimes unheated bathrooms challenging). In warm weather, however, it's a delightful treat.

Bamboo Garden Hotel
24 Xiaoshiqiao Hutong, Jiugulou Dajie, Xicheng District, 010-5852-0088; www.bbgh.com.cn
This attractive Qing-era courtyard boutique hotel is tucked into a hutong north of the Forbidden City and near the Drum Tower. Rooms are simple but clean and decorated with Chinese antiques and fabrics. The hotel has several restaurants serving Chinese specialties as well as a tea house, where guests can experience a Chinese tea ceremony while listening to live traditional music. *40 rooms. Restaurant, bar. Wireless Internet access. $*

Hotel Côté Cour SL
70 Yanyue Hutong, Dongcheng District, 010-6512-8020; www.hotelcotecoursl.com
This unique and luxurious court-

Bamboo Garden Hotel

Red Capital Club

yard hotel has 14 gorgeously decorated rooms swathed in luxury bedding, free wireless Internet and flat-screen TVs. Beautiful Chinese antiques fill the rooms, from the soft, early 20th-century rugs underfoot to the lacquered cabinets where you store your clothes. Breakfast is served in a luxurious dining room each morning (with everything from eggs to dim sum on the menu). Afternoon tea makes the spot a cozy gathering area. In warm weather, the courtyard is a peaceful place to lounge in the sun. The generous and friendly European owners will give tips on sightseeing in Beijing, whether it's how to get the best tickets to the opera or where to pick up contemporary artwork. Taxis have a hard time finding this spot, as it is tucked in a hutong in the Dongcheng district, but have the driver call the hotel and they'll graciously guide you. *14 rooms. Complimentary breakfast. Wireless Internet access. $$*

Red Capital Residence

9 Dongsi Liutiao, Dongcheng District, 010-8403-5308, 010-8401-8886 (reservations); www.redcapitalclub.com.cn
Tucked a few doors down from the Red Capital Club restaurant, this courtyard boutique hotel has just five rooms, each with period décor and names that play off the '50s-era Maoist theme of the hotel and restaurant (for example, the Chairman's suite or the two concubine's suites). In warm weather, the courtyard provides a romantic, idyllic spot for the breakfast that's included with the room rate. *5 rooms. Complimentary breakfast. $$*

Grand Hyatt

800-228-9548 (U.S.), 800-852-0230 (north China), 800-852-0231 (south China); www. beijing.grand.hyatt.com
A gleaming glass tower on busy Chang An Avenue, this large hotel delivers crisp, contemporary rooms with comfortable, duvet-topped beds and flat-screen TVs; a confident, friendly staff; and enough amenities and services to eliminate the need to leave the property. The fitness center and spa, Club Oasis, includes a sprawling, basement-level indoor pool that's a simulated fantasyland of palm trees, star-studded skies and waterfalls. On Saturday mornings, a member of the fitness staff guides willing guests on a 3K run of the city and rewards them with a complimentary T-shirt upon return. Made In China is one of the city's top and tastiest spots for Peking duck. The hotel is connected to the Oriental Plaza shopping mall and houses its own gallery of stores. *825 rooms. 5 restaurants, 2 bars. Indoor pool. Wireless Internet access. Business center. Spa. Fitness center. $$$*

★Novotel Peace Beijing

3 Jinyu Hutong (off Wangfujing Lu), Dongcheng District, 010-6512-8833; www.novotel.com
This budget-friendly hotel housed in a glass-clad tower offers a great location near Wangfujing shopping and the Forbidden City.

The recently renovated rooms are basic but feature flat-screen TVs and beds topped with down duvets. The hotel's restaurant, Le Cabernet, has classic French recipes and terrace seating in warm weather, while the Square, located off the lobby, offers a range of Western dishes 24 hours a day.

388 rooms. 2 restaurants, bar. Pool. Fitness center. $

★★★Park Plaza Beijing Wanfujing

97 Jinbao Jie, Dongcheng District, 010-8522-1999, 800-814-7000 (U.S.), 800-610-8886 (north China), 800-261-8888 (south China); www.parkplaza.com/beijingcn

Located next to the Regent Beijing and operated by the same owners, this new hotel offers crisp, comfortable rooms that are ideal for business travelers (the onsite Starbucks keeps guests caffeinated). Rooms are contemporary with flat-screen TVs, ample workspace and duvet-topped beds. The fitness center has the latest in treadmills and stationary bikes, and a massage center offers treatments from 10 a.m. to 2 a.m. Two onsite restaurants serve a variety of Asian specialties, from the fresh noodles at Oodle to the fried rice at Bloo.

216 rooms. 2 restaurants, bar. Wireless Internet access. Business center. Fitness center. $$

★★★★Peninsula Beijing

8 Jinyu Hutong (Goldfish Lane), Dongcheng District, 010-8516-2888, 800-852-3888 (north China), 800-152-3888 (south China); www.hshgroup.com

A prime location and above-and-beyond service make this upscale hotel a favorite of international business travelers. This was one of the first Western brands to debut in Beijing when it opened in 1989, and the hotel impressed with its multilevel gallery of über-luxury shops, including Harry Winston, Cartier, Chanel and more. Though the Peninsula's rooms are now ready for freshening up (with cramped bathrooms and small square footage totals), and at press time the fitness center and spa were closed for upgrading, the accommodating staff makes up for whatever the facilities may lack. Jing, the hotel's acclaimed contemporary restaurant serves updated Asian cuisine, while Huang Ting offers traditional Cantonese dishes in a setting designed to resemble a (very upscale) Qing-era courtyard with plenty of antique chairs, tables and accessories sourced from that era.

530 rooms. 2 restaurants, bar. Wireless Internet access. Airport transportation available. $$$

★★★★Raffles Beijing Hotel

33 Dongchangan Dajie, Dongcheng District, 010-6526-3388; www.beijing.raffles.com

This elegant, traditional hotel, housed in two buildings (one that dates to the 1900s and one that's a modern tower), has the city's most enviable location steps from Tiananmen Square, the Forbidden City and Wangfujiang's shopping. Rooms are swathed in romantic chintzes, oriental rugs and French furnishings but include contemporary touches like flat-screen TVs and DVD players on request. The staff is professional and accommodating and will do anything from providing a perfect cup of Earl Grey in the secluded, turn-of-the-century-inspired La Vie to providing a personalized wake-up call with fresh coffee on demand. Guests can lounge in the classic Writers Bar (named for the many famous authors who have stayed at the hotel) or dine at Jaan, the acclaimed onsite French restaurant. The hotel's fitness center is considered one of the capital city's best. *171 rooms. 3 restaurants, bar. Fitness center. Wireless Internet access. Airport transportation available. Pool. $$$*

★★★÷The Regent Beijing

99 Jinbao Jie, Dongcheng District, 010-8522-1888, 800-545-4000 (U.S.), 800-610-8888 (north China), 800-261-0306 (south China); www.regenthotels.com

Opened in 2005 in a newly constructed, contemporary tower that sits atop the Dengshikou subway stop, this hotel delivers a contemporary setting with Asian flair and prices that are a shade lower than those of its peers. Service here can be laid-back to the point

China World Hotel

of absent; you might find yourself flagging down waitstaff or a bellhop for help more often than not. Rooms are decorated in deep hues of aubergine and gold and have flat-screen TVs, duvet-topped beds and marble-clad bathrooms with deep soaking tubs. A spacious indoor pool and extensive fitness center with yoga studios keep guests fit, and the Serenity Spa stays open until 1 a.m. with a menu that includes acupuncture, traditional Swedish massage and more. Café 99 is a popular expat Sunday brunch haunt with a buffet loaded with Peking duck, sushi, salads and alluring desserts, and the price includes free-flowing Champagne or wine. The hotel's upscale Chinese restaurant, Lijing Xuan, is considered a top spot for Cantonese cuisine. *500 rooms. 4 restaurants, bar. Wireless Internet access. Spa. Pool. Airport transportation available. $$*

Chaoyang
★★Beijing News Plaza Hotel
26 Jianguomennei Dajie, Chaoyang District, 010-6521-1188
This recently built, Chinese-owned hotel is located off a busy stretch of road a few blocks from Tiananmen Square. Rooms are clean and comfortable with classic furnishings and marble bathrooms. The hotel caters to conferences and business meetings, so expect to see

suited travelers milling around the breakfast buffet or having evening cocktails in the lobby bar. Because it's a locally owned hotel, rooms here are often better priced than at similar Western-brand hotels. *201 rooms. 3 restaurants, 2 bars. Pool. Fitness center. Business center. Wireless Internet access. $$*

★★★÷China World Hotel
1 Jianguomenwai Dajie, Chaoyang District, 010-6505-2266, 866-565-5050 (U.S.), 800-852-5900 (north China), 800-152-5900 (south China); www.shangri-la.com/chinaworld/
Splashed in bold red hues and plenty of gilded accents, this hotel, which is managed by Shangri-La, brings old-school Chinese glamour to a modern setting above the China World Center shopping center. Rooms have flat-screen TVs, duvet-topped beds, workspaces with Herman Miller chairs and unique touches like a pillow menu and marble baths. The Lobby Lounge, with its Chinese antiques and fabrics and live piano music, is an elegant spot for tea or cocktails. A sprawling fitness center has squash courts, an indoor pool, table tennis, an aerobics studio with a full menu of classes, and indulgent locker rooms with saunas and steam rooms. *716 rooms. 5 restaurants, bar. Business center. Pool. Spa. Fitness center. $$$*

★★★Great Wall Sheraton Hotel Beijing

10 Dongsanhuan Beilu, Chaoyang District, 010-6590-5566, 800-325-3535; www.starwoodhotels.com

Located just outside the third ring road next to the National Agriculture Exhibition Center, the Great Wall Sheraton is a bit far from the hustle and bustle of the main intersections but still strategically located to provide a convenient stay. The hotel looks much older than others in the area with a fading traditional Chinese interior, but it more than does the trick for business stays. The hotel offers all the basic amenities, including a 24-hour business center, gym and indoor heated pool. For a more luxurious stay, book a room on the Elite floor.

827 rooms. 3 restaurants, 2 bars. Pool. Fitness center. Business center. Wireless Internet access. $$

★★★Hilton Beijing

1 Dongfang Lu, Dongsanhuan Beilu, Chaoyang District, 010-5865-5000; www.beijing.hilton.com

Located near the business district about 20 minutes from the airport, the Hilton Beijing is perfect for business travelers. It has all the essentials, including a full-service business center, Internet-ready rooms, and five restaurants and bars. Strategic use of red—a lucky color in Chinese culture—and traditional Chinese window detailing add some ethnic flair to the otherwise standard hotel design. A minor restoration completed in 2006 included replacing the carpet and renovating the lobby, but the age of the hotel still shows. A brand-new executive tower is set to be completed and open before summer 2008. The currently incomplete structures across the street will be new embassies.

340 rooms. Wireless Internet access. 3 restaurants, 2 bars. Airport transportation available. Fitness center. Pool. Business center. $$$

★★★Hotel Kunlun

2 Xinyuannan Lu, Chaoyang District, 010-6590-3388; www.hotelkunlun.com/en/

The Hotel Kunlun's great location means it's often booked. One of the more spacious hotels in the Embassy Area, it boasts 10 restaurants, each exquisitely designed to provide a distinctive dining experience. The Japanese restaurant, Keikoku, is modeled after a traditional fishing village, and entirely transports you to another land. The Sunshine Lounge's full-length windows overlook the hotel's grassy areas, and the high ceilings provide an elegant atmosphere. The fitness center looks new, and there's also an onsite beauty salon and spa. Be sure to visit the mar-

Hotel Kunlun

ket across the street for souvenirs. *764 rooms. 8 restaurants, 3 bars. Complimentary breakfast buffet. Fitness center. $$*

★★★Hotel New Otani Chang Fu Gong

26 Jianguomenwai Dajie, Chaoyang District, 010-6512-5555
Housed in a new, modern tower off Chang An Avenue, this hotel, a joint venture between the Chinese and the Japanese group behind New Otani hotels, has clean, basic rooms, a full-service spa, and a fitness center that offers sports from basketball to table tennis. The hotel includes Japanese, Chinese and Western restaurants, as well as an onsite cake shop that churns out superb cakes, breads and pastries baked fresh daily. *500 rooms. 4 restaurants, bar.*

Fitness center. High-speed Internet access. Business center. $$

★★★Kempinski Hotel Beijing Lufthansa Center

50 Liangmaqiao Lu, Chaoyang District, 010-6465-3388; www.kempinski-beijing.com
Connected to the Beijing Lufthansa Center, the Kempinski provides easy access to shopping and numerous restaurants, which cater to every taste with cuisines from around the world. A full-service business center and travel agency are located in the lobby, making it convenient for guests to make plans. The hotel is also within an easy distance of tourist sites. Although the exterior looks shabby, the interior is new and has a contemporary European design. The rooms

PHOTO: COURTESY HOTEL KUNLUN

aren't as impressive as the lobby areas, but the on-par service helps ensure a pleasant stay.

526 rooms. High-speed Internet access. 7 restaurants, 2 bars. Airport transportation available. Fitness center. Pool. Business center. $$$

★★★Kerry Centre Hotel

1 Guanghua Lu, Chaoyang District, 010-6561-8833, 866-565-5050 (U.S.), 800-852-5900 (north China), 800-152-5900 (south China); www.shangri-la.com/kerrycentre

With its prime location in the Chaoyang district, this hotel is a great choice for business travelers. The Kerry Centre is managed by the Shangri-La group, which means that service is a shade more attentive than at traditional business hotels. Rooms are streamlined and contemporary, with duvet-topped beds and flat-screen TVs. The lobby bar, Centro, is packed nightly thanks to its Western-style cocktails and live entertainment—the clientele is a fashionable mix of stylish locals and visiting expats.

487 rooms. Restaurant, bar. Wireless Internet access. Fitness center. Business center. $$$

★★★Renaissance Beijing Hotel

36 Xiaoyun Lu, Chaoyang District, 010-6468-9999, 800-468-3571; www.renaissancehotels.com

Even though the Renaissance is situated on the bustling street of Xiaoyun Lu, the hotel is set back far enough to provide a quiet stay—and it's still within walking distance of Sanlitun, a hub of Beijing nightlife. Shopping centers are also close by, as are restaurants and other eateries that stay open late into the night. When you're not shopping or out on the town, the hotel has a serene atmosphere, and the service is impeccable. The indoor pool is beautiful and designed with a Greek influence, though the fitness center is small. All in all, the Renaissance is carefully managed, as evidenced by its clean and shiny interior, which fuses Chinese design into a contemporary setting.

218 rooms. 2 restaurants, bar. High-speed Internet access. $$

★★★★St. Regis Hotel Beijing

21 Jianguomenwai Dajie, Chaoyang District, 010-6460-6688; www.stregis.com

The grande dame of Beijing hotels, this classically elegant property, which was renovated in early 2008, delivers white-glove service from arrival to departure. The concierge staff is particularly adept at arranging car services or tours and can steer you to the city's best shops and restaurants. Twice-daily butler ser-

Ritz-Carlton Beijing

Swissotel Beijing

vice keeps the rooms sparkling and neat, from fresh flowers in the bedroom to fluffy, high-quality towels in the marble-clad bathrooms. The fitness center includes an indoor pool, classes such as tai chi and yoga, and 24-hour access to the squash courts and putting range. Dining options within the hotel include Danieli, an upscale Italian dining room, and the Astor Grill, which offers alfresco dining in summer months. *273 rooms. 4 restaurants, 4 bars. Spa. Fitness center. High-speed Internet access. $$$$*

★★★Sofitel Wanda Beijing

93 Jianguo Lu, Tower C Wanda Plaza, Chaoyang District, 010-8599-6666; www.sofitel.com

A striking marriage of French and Asian style, this high-rise hotel is a calm oasis off busy Jianguo Road. The location, a long walk between two subway stops, and constant traffic makes getting around town more challenging, but the rooms and public areas are stylish enough to make you forget leaving the hotel. Rooms feature plush beds, romantic Asian fabrics and Art Deco–inspired furniture. Bathrooms are decked out with marble tubs with their own TVs and spacious showers with rain shower heads. Le Spa offers a full menu of massages, facials and salon services and access to a relaxing, private indoor pool. An international cinema is a convenient distraction, and Beijing's first Wal-Mart is nearby in case you've forgotten anything from home. *417 rooms. Wireless Internet access. 4 restaurants, 2 bars. Business center. Spa. Fitness center. $$$*

★★Swissôtel Beijing

2 Chaoyangmen Bei Dajie, Chaoyang District, 010-6553-2288; www.beijing.swissotel.com

Rooms at this business hotel are perfectly Swiss—comfortable and efficient, but frills-free. The ultra-neutral, beige-and-blond wood rooms feature duvet-topped beds. The location next to a subway stop makes getting around the city easy. The fitness center and spa are open to employees in the hotel's office complex, the Hong Kong Macau Center, and because of the public access, they are far from fancy. *430 rooms. 3 restaurants, 2 bars. Fitness center. Pool. High-speed Internet access. $$$*

★★Traders Hotel

1 Jianguomenwai Dajie, Chaoyang District, 010-6505-2277, 866-565-5050 (U.S.), 800-852-5900 (north China), 800-152-5900 (south China); www.shangri-la.com

Ritz-Carlton Financial Street

Shangri-La manages this business-targeted hotel, so service is attentive and efficient. Rooms are contemporary with Asian accents, and they feature comfortable, plush beds, minibars and satellite TV. While Traders has its own fitness and sauna facilities, guests of the hotel can also use the fitness center and spa facilities at the sister property, the China World Hotel, reachable by the underground China World shopping center. *549 rooms. 2 restaurants, bar. High-speed Internet access. $$*

Xicheng District
★★★Intercontinental Beijing Financial Street
11 Jinrong Jie, Xicheng District, 010-5852-5888, 888-424-6835; www.intercontinental.com/icbeijing
A gleaming Financial Street tower is the setting for this sparkling business hotel. Rooms have contemporary décor with earth tones and warm wood accents. Amenities include flat-screen TVs, DVD players, on-call butler service and in-room stereos. Visiting executives flock to the I-Spa, which has saunas, whirlpools and a full range of spa ser-

vices, or to the fitness center, which is stocked with Lifecycles, Stairmasters and treadmills.

332 rooms. 4 restaurants, bar. Wireless Internet access. Fitness center. Spa. Business center. $$

★★★✦Ritz-Carlton Financial Street

1 Jin Cheng Fan St. E., Beijing, Xicheng District, 10-6601-6666; www.ritzcarlton.com

Dramatic and contemporary, this luxury hotel in the city's newly constructed Financial Street area is poised to become of the city's top places to stay once a few wrinkles in service are ironed out. Rooms are loaded with high-tech amenities, including bedside control panels for the automated blinds, flat-screen TVs, iPod docking stations and even a separate TV for the bathroom. The lobby lounge, attended by waitresses in canary-yellow Mandarin-style dresses and decorated with rich Chinese silks and antique birdcages, is a stylish spot for tea or a cocktail. The onsite Italian restaurant, Cepe, is considered the city's top spot for new Italian cooking and features a dramatic, color-splashed modern design. A basement-level fitness center boasts a lap pool crowned by a movie screen on which the staff plays classic film noir or the picture of your choice.

253 rooms. 4 restaurants, bar. Wireless Internet access. Spa. Fitness center. Business center. $$$

Haidian District

★★★★Shangri-La Hotel Beijing

29 Zizhuyuan Lu, Haidian District, 010-6841-2211, 866-565-5050 (U.S.), 800-852-5900 (north China), 800-152-5900 (south China); www.shangri-la.com

With warm lighting and classic décor, the Shangri-La is easily one of Beijing's top hotels (though travelers should take note of its remote location near the Summer Palace—trips to the city center could take up to an hour in traffic). Its elegant design features Chinese detailing, including wooden panels that resemble traditional Chinese windows. Mirrored ceilings give hallways a spacious feeling. The newly added Valley Wing features rooms that are even more spacious and elegant than those in the Garden Wing and include perks like butler service. The well-equipped gym; relaxing pool area; and new, world-class spa ensure your stay will be more than comfortable. The restaurants offer plenty of variety, from the famous Blu Lobster to the newly remodeled Nishimura. The Chinese-influenced rooftop gardens,

Traders

which are connected to the gym facilities, are perfect for strolling. Located farther from the city center, the Shangri-La helps guests find serenity in their stay. *660 rooms. 4 restaurants, 4 bars. Airport transportation available. Fitness center. Pool. Business Center. Wireless Internet access. $$$*

★★★Westin Beijing Financial Street

9B Jinrong Jie, Xicheng District, 010-6606-8866, 800-937-8461 (U.S.), 800 988 3688 (China); www.westin.com
Opened in 2007, this modern hotel housed in a new tower on Financial Street is a popular choice for business and leisure travelers because of its full range of amenities and bargain room rates. Rooms feature the chain's signature Heavenly beds and fluffy duvets as well as complimentary wireless Internet access. The spa is a soothing, candlelit retreat where guests can try massages, facials or salon services. The hotel has four restaurants, which serve everything from Italian food (at Prego) to contemporary Chinese (Jewel). Shui Bar serves "health elixirs" from the spa menu.

Shangra-La Hotel

PHOTO: COURTESY SHANGRA-LA HOTEL

486 rooms. 4 restaurants, 3 bars. Wireless Internet access. Fitness center. Spa. $$

On the horizon

The following hotels were either too recently opened at press time to receive a star rating or were due for completion in 2008. Travelers to Beijing will quickly learn that a new hotel is opening in the capital city just about every week, and the variety and choice of rooms will only increase in the future. Here, a sampling of the best of the new:

Fairmont Beijing
Chaoyang District, 800-441-1414; www.fairmont.com
The first outpost in China for this Canadian hotel brand will feature luxuriously appointed rooms, top-notch service and a location in Beijing's newly burgeoning central business district. The hotel is slated to open summer 2008.
235 rooms. Restaurants, bars. Spa. Fitness center. Business center.

JW Marriott Hotel Beijing
83 Jianguo Lu, Chaoyang District, 010-5908-6688, 888-236-2427 (U.S.), 400-888-5551 (China); www.marriott.com

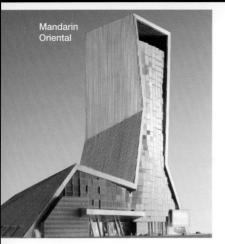

Mandarin Oriental

Opened in November 2007, this business-oriented hotel is wired for today with high-speed Internet, iPod docking stations in each room and oversized flat-screen TVs. Rooms are light and airy with plush bedding and contemporary bathrooms with their own flat-screen TVs. The exclusive Shin Kong Place and China Central Place shopping malls are adjacent.
549 rooms. 3 restaurants, 2 bars. Fitness center. Wireless Internet access.

Mandarin Oriental, Beijing

1 Hu Jia Lou, Xinyuan Jie, Chaoyang District, 010-5906-1888, 866-526-6567 (U.S.), 800-852-0241 (China); www.mandarinoriental.com/beijing/
It's hard to miss the new, ultra-futuristic Rem Koolhaas– designed China Central TV headquarters that's taking shape in the city's Central Business District. Critics complain that the unique shape of the building looks like a person kneeling, which is a symbol of defeat; proponents applaud the building's unique double-L design, a feat of engineering magic. The Mandarin Oriental, which will be housed in an adjacent building that's part of the new complex, is scheduled to open before the end of 2008. Expect over-the-top luxury throughout, from the cutting-edge guest rooms to the much-anticipated, super-indulgent spa.
241 rooms. 3 restaurants, 3 bars. Wireless Internet access. Spa. Fitness center. Business center.

The Opposite House

11 Sanlitun Rd., Chaoyang Distrcit, 010-6417-6688; www.boardroomcollection.net
For those who want to stay near the city's top nightlife in style comes this Japanese-designed boutique hotel set in the middle of the Sanlitun Bar area. Rooms are modern and minimalist, with Chinese antiques added to the mix for a sense of balance. Look for creature comforts like iPod docking stations, deep oak soaking tubs and flat-screen TVs.
99 rooms. Restaurant, bar. Wireless Internet access. Fitness center. Spa.

Park Hyatt Beijing

2 Jianguomenwai Dajie, Beijing Yintai Centre, Chaoyang District, 010-8567-1234, 800-228-9548 (U.S.), 800-852-0230 (north China), 800-152-0230 (south China); www.beijing.park.hyatt.com/
Designed for those who love cutting-edge creature comforts, this hotel will feature contemporary, soothingly neutral rooms with spa bathrooms outfitted with rain showers, heated floors and yards of limestone. The hotel is set to open mid-2008.
237 rooms. 3 restaurants, 4 bars. Spa. Fitness center. Business center. Wireless Internet access.

Ritz-Carlton Beijing

83A Jianguo Lu, Chaoyang District, 010-5908-8888, 800-542-8680 (U.S.), 800-600-0666 (north China), 800-260-0666 (south China); www.ritzcarlton.com
Unveiled in December 2007, this gorgeous Chaoyang hotel offers English colonial style and top-notch service for an utterly civilized, pampering stay. No detail has been overlooked in the elegant rooms, which feature hardwood floors, marble-clad baths (the thoughtfully placed flat-screen TV near the bathtub means you won't miss a minute of CNN updates), and Bulgari bath products. Even the wiring is smart: the heating and cooling system "senses" when a guest is present and adjusts the temperature accordingly, and the shades and draperies operate from a bedside panel. A wedding chapel was included, the luxe Shin Kong Place shopping center is adjacent to the hotel, and the new JW Marriott is connected by an underground passageway.
305 rooms. 4 restaurants, bar. Wireless Internet access. Spa. Fitness center. Business center. Pool.

Westin Beijing Chaoyang

1-3 Xinyuannan Lu, Chaoyang District, 010-6466-5949, 800-937-8461 (U.S.), 800-988-3688 (China); www.westinchaoyangdistrict.com
Look for the signature Westin touches when this Financial Street location opens in summer 2008. That means super-comfortable Heavenly beds; cutting-edge technology, from wireless Internet to flat-screen TVs; and a Heavenly Spa with sprawling spa suites for private pampering.
558 rooms. Restaurants, bar. Spa. Pool. Fitness center. Business center. Wireless Internet access.

BEIJING

DINING

PHOTO: COURTESY REGENT HOTEL

CUISINES
AROUND CHINA

You can find restaurants throughout the capital city serving dishes from just about every part of China, but don't let that intimidate you. Food is a central part of Chinese culture, and with a little know-how, you can navigate from spicy Sichuan dishes to the sour and spicy food of Guizhou. HERE'S A GUIDE.

BEIJING Drawing from all over China (as emperors of different dynasties all had the best cooks from every region come to prepare meals), Beijing cuisine has also influenced other Chinese cuisines. It's sometimes difficult to tell where a dish originated (the term Mandarin refers not only to Beijing but other provinces as well). Beijing meals are often served as small bites rather than full courses, and frying is a popular cooking method with lots of dark soy sauce, sesame oil and scallions often thrown into the mix. Typical dishes include Peking duck, hot-and-sour soup, mutton hot pot, beggar's chicken and dumplings.

SHANGHAI A hallmark of Shanghai cuisine is the use of alcohol and sugar. Fish, chicken and crab are dunked in alcohol and then cooked or served raw. Sugar is often combined with soy sauce

to give a savory flavor. A popular dish is sweet-and-sour spare ribs. The cuisine is also known for delicate buns called xiaolong mantou.

CANTONESE Most Chinese restaurants in the West serve this regional cuisine from the southern province now called Guangdong, which is very diverse and incorporates just about any meat you can think of. Ginger, soy sauce, rice wine, sesame and garlic are used for flavor, and stir-fry is a popular cooking method. A number of noodle dishes are also part of Cantonese cuisine, including wonton noodles. Desserts include shaved ice and wild rice with coconut milk.

XINJIANG This cuisine from far northwestern China is known for lamb kebobs and noodles. A popular dish is lagman, or boiled handmade noodles with beef,

Dining in Beijing

lamb or vegetables. Most people probably know this cuisine by the nutty flatbread called naan.

SHANXI This northern cuisine is known for noodles; fried flatbread called da bing; and a sour taste, often derived from locally produced vinegar.

SICHUAN This food from southwestern China is known for being numbingly hot thanks to Sichuan peppercorns and red chilies. The plant grows in the hot, humid Sichuan province. But not all Sichuan is scorching. Typical dishes include kung pao chicken and dan dan noodles.

TAIWAN Seafood figures prominently in Taiwanese cuisine. Pork is also popular, but beef is less so (since some Buddhists are reluctant to eat it). Soy sauce, rice wine, peanuts, chili peppers, cilantro, fermented black beans and pickled radishes are all commonly used for flavoring. Bubble tea (which includes balls of tapioca) is from Taiwan.

GUIZHOU Dishes from this southwestern province are sour and spicy. A popular element is a salt-picked vegetable called yan cai.

YUNNAN Quite spicy, this cuisine from the southwestern corner of China, abutting Vietnam, Laos and Myanmar (Burma), frequently includes edible flowers and mushrooms.

What to Eat

Chinese culture values food and eating; in fact, gaining weight has been seen as a sign of wealth and prosperity. The exquisite dining experience wasn't always easy to find in Beijing. Today, however, non-Chinese restaurants aim high (and sometimes miss the mark in cuisines like Italian or French), but the growing number of for-eigners in the city—both expa-triates and tourists—has fueled a boom in variety. Restaurants around the city serve a variety of Chinese cooking, from the signa-ture dishes of the Xinjiang region near Tibet to the fiery-hot food of areas like Sichuan. Now, with star chefs at the helm of both Western and Chinese restaurants, a satis-fying meal isn't hard to come by.

Chaoyang District
Alameda

Sanlitun Houjie (beside Nali Mall), Tongli Studios, Chaoyang District, 010-6417-8084

One of the most popular restau-rants in Beijing since its open-ing in 2005, Alameda proves that Brazilian cuisine delivers more than just barbecued meats. The menu includes traditional Brazilian dishes like feijoada (black bean and smoked meat stew) and oth-ers with European flair. The menu changes daily to highlight the freshest ingredients. Located near the embassies, Alameda provides a tasty and affordable business lunch and a nice place to relax in an airy, greenhouse-like space.
Brazilian menu. Lunch, dinner. $$

Aria Bar and Restaurant

2/F, China World Hotel, 1 Jianguomenwai Dajie, 010-6505-2266, Chaoyang District; www.shangri-la.com/en/prop-erty/beijing/chinaworld

From the chic bar of this restau-rant in the China World Hotel, the signature spiral staircase leads to an elegant, warmly lit dining room. It's a comfort-able spot from which to enjoy European cuisine such as wild halibut or venison ravioli. The extensive selection of fine wine draws expats to the bar and dining room, and the bang-for-your-yuan lunch menus make this a prime power lunch spot.
International menu. Lunch, Monday-Friday; Dinner daily. $$

Asian Star

26 Dongsanhuan Bei Lu, Chaoyang District, 010-6582-5306/1717

Don't be fooled by the small storefront: this unpretentious restaurant offers a large array of dishes in a variety of cuisines, including Indian, Malaysian, Singaporean and Thai. An open area lets patrons watch the chef hand-toss the naan—both plain

Baskets of steaming dumplings

and garlic—which is then served cut up in baskets, fresh and piping hot. The kitchen does a good job with the basics, like the palak paneer, butter chicken and tom yung kung soup. The Lhasa milk tea is full-bodied and flavorful without being too sweet.
Pan-Asian menu. Lunch, dinner. $

Bellagio (Lu Gang Xiaozhen)

35 Xiaoyun Lu (opposite Renaissance Hotel), Chaoyang District, 010-8451-9988;
6 Gongti Xi Lu (South of Gongti 100 bowling alley), Chaoyang District, 010-6551-3533
The beef stew noodles and stewed, shredded beef with rice at this popular café-style hangout are authentic Taiwanese, but treats from other parts of China also are served here, including Cantonese-style snacks like coconut milk with tapioca. The Shin Kong Place location isn't a late-night hangout like the other two, but it is newer and delivers more stylish décor. Close to the city's nightlife centers, the Xiaoyun Lu and Gongti Xi Lu locations are perfect for late-night snacking.
Taiwan menu. Lunch, dinner. $

Chuan Ban

5 Gongyuan Toutiao, Jianguomennei Dajie, Chaoyang District, 010-6512-2277
The city's most popular (and afford-

able) Sichuan restaurant is one of the best places in the city to numb your tongue with fiery hot food. The piquant fish (shuizhuyu) and smoked duck are popular with the crowds who flock here throughout the day.
Sichuan. Lunch, dinner. $

Comptoirs de France Bakery

Room 102, 1/F, Building 15, China Central Place, 89 Jianguo Lu, Chaoyang District, 010-6530-5480;
East Lake Villa, 35 Dongzhimenwai Dajie, 010-6461-1525; www.comptoirsdefrance.com
Opened by two Frenchmen, Comptoirs de France sells authentic French delicacies, from macaroons to pastries to all sorts of breads. For a Chinese twist, try the chocolate Sichuan pepper macaroon or Sichuan hot chocolate. The quiches, sandwiches, éclairs and croissants are all tasty, and the hot chocolates and homemade ice cream draw crowds. The contemporary, dark wood interior is classic and provides a nice café environment to enjoy the exquisite food.
French menu. Breakfast, lunch, dinner. $$

Din Tai Fung

24 Xinyuanxili Zhongjie, Chaoyang District, 010-6462-4502;
6F Shin Kong Place, 87 Jianguo Lu, Chaoyang District (inside Shin Kong Place), 010-6533-1536;
www.dintaifung.com.cn
The original Taiwan location of this

Peking Duck

A TRADITIONAL DINNER of Beijing's most famous dish is a must during your visit. Peking duck was first prepared for the Emperor of China in the Yuan Dynasty, which began in 1271. Today, it's considered one of China's national foods and is often prepared for visiting dignitaries. You've probably had duck in a Chinese restaurant, but Peking duck has a specific preparation. Ducks are specially bred for the dish—they are given plenty of food and kept sedentary to fatten them up. Before cooking, air is pumped into the duck to separate the skin. Afterward, the skin is ladled with boiling water to make it drier and brushed with a sugar-water syrup to give it a rich amber color. The duck is then hung and dried for several hours before it's roasted in a closed oven or hung over a fire. Authentic restaurants carve the duck in front of you and serve the skin first, which should be thin and crispy; sugar and garlic sauce is used for dipping. The meat is eaten with pancakes (called bing in Chinese), scallions and hoisin sauce and served with vegetables such as cucumber. The idea is to roll it all up—and dig in. While you eat the duck, the trimmings are sometimes made into a soup, which is served as a second course. A number of restaurants in Beijing specialize in Peking duck, including Li Qun, Da Dong and Made in China, and the best require reservations so that your duck can be roasted and ready to eat when you arrive.

Green T. House

PHOTO: COURTESY GREEN T. HOUSE

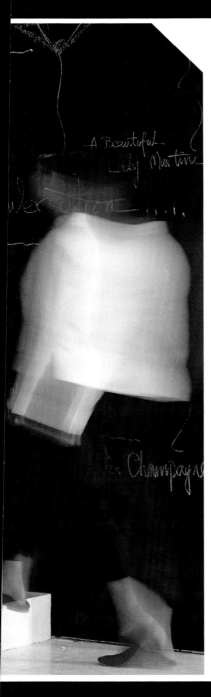

Shanghai cuisine restaurant was once named one of the top 10 restaurants in the world by the *New York Times*. Now, there are two locations in Beijing, with one newly opened in the chic Shin Kong shopping center. Fashionable Beijingers come to Din Tai Fung to feast on its famous Shanghai-style dumplings filled with hot soup. Other menu standouts include the vegetable and meat dumplings as well as noodle dishes like dan dan mian (noodles in peanut and sesame sauce) and beef stew noodles. Finish your meal with either a traditional dessert, like mini steamed buns filled with red bean paste, or something more contemporary, like almond jelly and shaved ice served with condensed milk.
Shanghai menu. Lunch, dinner. $

Da Dong Roast Duck Restaurant

Building 3, Tuanjiehu Beikou, Dongsanhuan Lu (southeast corner of Changhong Qiao), Chaoyang District, 010-6582-2892/4003; Building 1-2, Nanxincang Guoji Dasha (Tower), A22 Dongsishitiao, Dongcheng District, 010-5169-0329

How will you have your duck? With some sauce and duck tucked into a special bun? With some shredded cucumber and radish? Or, like the Empress Dowager Cixi, by dunking some crisply fried duck skin in chunky granules of sugar?

Regardless of how you choose to eat your duck, Da Dong provides all the requisite condiments in an upscale environment, especially at its newer location in Nanxincang (the first location near the Sanlitun area remains a well-known tourist destination). The exquisite décor and modern interior aren't the only reasons to check out the new location—it's situated next to the city's old grain storage buildings, adding that much more culture to the experience. The open-view kitchen allows guests to watch the chefs expertly roast the birds and drain the finished ducks' fat. There are some innovative dishes on the menu, but it's best to stick with traditional fare, such as Peking duck, Chinese cabbage cooked with chestnuts and duck wings.
Beijing menu. Lunch, dinner. $

Green T. House (Zi Yun Xuan)

6 Gongti Xi Lu, Chaoyang District, 010-6552-8310/8311; www.green-t-house.com
This trendy, ultra-hip restaurant also serves as an art gallery. The fusion dishes (think green-tea dumplings) are more novel than spectacular, but the visual feast makes up for any mediocrity of flavor. There's a wide selection of teas and an opportunity to browse the artworks on offer. Expect to spend, but

you'll enjoy your experience.
Chinese menu. Lunch, dinner. $$

Haiku by Hatsune

Block 8 Complex, No. 8 Chaoyang Park West Road, Chaoyang District, 010-6508-8585; www.block8.cn/index.htm
Often less crowded than its popular sister restaurant Hatsune, Haiku provides a calmer, swankier atmosphere in which to enjoy your California and spicy tuna rolls. Beijing's star chef Alan Wong is behind the extensive menu of sashimi and sushi, which showcases everything from roasted sea conch to Kobe beef rolls. After dinner, stop in at Haiku's Block 8 neighbors, iUltra Lounge and Med Grill.
Sushi menu. Dinner. $$

Hatsune

2/F, Heqiao Building C, A8 Guanghua Dong Lu, Chaoyang District, 010-6581-3939
Reservations are recommended at this stylish hangout, which is especially popular with expats craving a California roll fix. The 119 roll—tuna with a special sauce—is imaginative and fresh, and the Beijing roll of roast duck and sauce is unique. Basics like sashimi and tempura are perfectly executed, and the extensive sake menu does not disappoint.

Haiku by Hatsune

Sushi menu. Lunch, dinner. $$

Huajia Yiyuan

5 Dongzhimen Nei Dajie,
010-8407-5288;
235 Dongzhimennei Dajie (near
Gui Jie), 010-6405-1908;
8 Dongdaqiao Lu, 5/F Shangdu
SOHO West Building, Chaoyang
District, 010-5900-3055
To enjoy contemporary Chinese
cuisine in a cozy courtyard set-
ting (with occasional live tradi-
tional music), visit the original
Gui Je location of this restaurant
trio. If you prefer dining in a more
modern environment, head to the
newer branch. The menu here is

varied and includes everything
from spicy crayfish to green draft
beer (drunk for good health).
Contemporary Chinese
menu. Lunch, dinner. $

I Rock My Pot

37-38 Chaowai Dajie, Chaoyang
District, 010-5879-0999
This hot pot eatery boasts a
condiment bar of almost 20
sauces for creating your own
dipping concoction. Dunk
your self-cooked sweet pota-
toes, shiitake mushrooms, os-
trich meat, seafood mush and
fish balls (or whatever else you
choose to order) into the boil-

Sushi at Haiku by Hatsune

ing broth of your choice, from curry to traditional Sichuan. Shiny silver curtains and high-backed red chairs lend some flare to the experience.

Hot pot. Lunch, dinner. $

Jasmine Restaurant and Lounge

Gongti Dong Lu (opposite Gate No. 9 of Worker's Stadium), Chaoyang District, 010-6553-8608/6553-8609; www.beijingjasmine.com

Housed in a building that looks something like a fortress on the outside and a sleek, contemporary supper club on the inside (with crystal chandeliers; plush, white futuristic arm-chairs; and a multistory atrium), Jasmine serves fusion food with Cantonese and Southeast Asian influences. The Kobe beef with foie gras and the Kyoto roasted cod reflect the idea of using sauces to heighten a food's traditional Cantonese flavor. Order the cheese panna cotta with strawberry sauce for a rich finish to a memorable meal. The stylish terrace is perfect for warm days.

Contemporary Chinese menu. Lunch, dinner. $$

Jin Ding Xuan

16 Pufang Lu, Fang Zhuang, Fengtai District, 010-6761-7161; 15 Tuanjiehu Nan Lu, Chaoyang District, 010-8596-8881;

PHOTO: COURTESY HAIKU BY HATSUNE

15 Anjui Bei Li (east of Fifth Avenue),
Olympic Area, 010-6497-8978;
77 Heping Xijie, Yonghegong,
Chaoyang District, 010-6429-6888
Who can say no to 24-hour dim sum? Perfect for those late-night cravings, the dim sum at Jin Ding Xuan is basic and cheap. There aren't any carts loaded with choose-your-own-dumplings here, but there's still plenty to select from, including shu mai (pork dumplings), chicken feet and spare ribs with black bean sauce. The multistoried, neon-lit exterior hints at the rowdiness inside.
Dim sum. Open 24 hours. $

La Galerie Restaurant
Ritan Park, South Gate, Guanghua Lu,
Chaoyang District, 010-8563-8698
Housed in a beautiful, traditional Chinese courtyard structure, La Galerie may look like an expensive tourist trap, but the Cantonese cuisine here is outstanding (albeit higher priced than that of its competitors). The barbecue pork pastries are sinfully rich, crispy and deliver a flavorful softness with each bite, while the superb egg tarts have a flaky crust and are filled with perfectly sweet and smooth custard. With a prime location overlooking Ritan Park, La Galerie is an alfresco favorite in warmer weather.
Cantonese menu. Lunch, dinner. $$

Lu Lu
1A Ziyunsi Lu, Chaoyang District,
010-6508-0101/0505
This sprawling, glitzy restaurant serves some of the best Shanghai dishes in the city, and most are relatively affordable if you stick with the basics, like the sweet-and-sour spare ribs. The simple buns, served both steamed and fried, come with condensed milk as a dipping sauce and are satisfyingly delicious. The fried radish buns are flaky and golden with a perfect sesame-crusted bottom. If you're feeling adventurous, try the popular, freshly "squeezed" corn juice. Stay away from the non-Shanghai dishes, which may not be worth the price. The restaurant also has many rooms of varying sizes for private dinners or business meetings.
Shanghai menu. Lunch, dinner. $$

Mare
14 Xindong Lu, Chaoyang District,
010-6416-5431/6417-1459;
Ground Floor, E-Tower, 12
Guanghua Lu, Guomao District,
010-6595-4178/2890
It used to be that you couldn't find a decent Spanish restaurant in Beijing. Mare fills that gap with an extensive tapas menu, with many items catering to vegetarians. Locals complain that the food isn't entirely authentic, but the popular chocolate lava cake

Salt

might just make up for any short-comings. Mare's set lunches are a great value. If nothing else, swing by for some coffee and dessert.
Spanish menu. Lunch, dinner. $$

Na Jia Xiaoguan

Jianguomenwai Dajie (west side of Middle School No. 119), Yongan Li, Chaoyang District, 010-6567-3663/6568-6553
This simple yet elegant restaurant delivers Manchurian cuisine with a punch. The space is intricate and carefully thought-out, and the menu doesn't come in a typical bound book—instead, the names of dishes are carved onto small planks of wood and "served" on a tray. The crispy fried shrimp

keep locals coming back for more, but the mashed potatoes, eggplant, sour plum juice and corn juice are also standouts.
Chinese menu. Lunch, dinner. $

Noodle Loft (Mian Ku)

20 Xi Dawang Lu, Chaoyang District, 010-6774-9950/5372; 3 Heping Xijie, Chaoyang District, 010-5130-9655
This stylish Shanxi-style noodle parlor elevates noodle making to an art. A team of chefs prepares the noodles from scratch from a central bar stocked with bubbling pots of water. Seeing them per-form such feats as preparing the long-life noodles (one continuous string of noodle rumored to be

PHOTO: COURTESY SALT

as long as 20 feet) is entertainment in itself. Stick with the more popular dishes like cat's ears noodles (shaped like mini feline ears) dipped in stewed beef, or youmian (rolled-up pieces of thin noodle) served with three dipping sauces: a sour, tomato-based sauce with pieces of scrambled egg; a mutton-based sauce; and a vinegar-based sauce. The modern and clean décor is simple, and the prices are amazingly low.
Shanxi menu. Lunch, dinner. $

Olio

77-79 Jianguo Lu, B124 China Central Place (basement of Shin Kong Place), Chaoyang District, 010-6530-7882; www.olio.sg/outlet-oliobeijing.asp
This Singaporean restaurant's Beijing outpost is located in the basement of office and shopping complex China Central Place, which is connected to the basement of the equally luxe mall Shin Kong Place (you'll find shops of every brand from Gucci to Ferragamo). The soft-shell crab sandwich and the tandoori chicken sandwich are favorites with locals, who come to the area to shop. The bread is made by a local bakery using a traditional Singaporean recipe, and dishes such as Nonya-style chicken rice and the Hainan chicken rice are equally authen-

tic. Desserts are simple but satisfying and half-priced every day from 2 p.m. to 6 p.m. The clean, modern interior, great prices and ultra-friendly Singaporean waitstaff are all icing on the cake.
Singaporean menu. Lunch, dinner. $$$

Pinot Brasserie

1/F, JW Marriott Hotel, 83 Jianguo Lu, China Central Place, Chaoyang District, 010-5908-6688; www.marriott.com/bjsjw
In the new JW Marriott Hotel, Pinot Brasserie is every bit a traditional French brasserie (case in point: the extensive pinot noir and pinot gris menu). Inside, Art Deco details accent the clean interior, and the open kitchen provides patrons a peek into the French chef's domain. Patio seating can also be enjoyed on good days. The mashed potatoes are particularly creamy and delicious and make an ideal accompaniment to any entrée.
French menu. Lunch, dinner. $

Phrik Thai

1/F, Gateway Building, 10 Yabao Lu, Chaoyang District, 010-8561-5236
Located in a Chaoyang office building and popular with working people nearby, this restaurant is a good choice for Thai food. The fish baked in foil retains all its juices, and the accompanying dipping sauce is spicy but

flavorful, perfectly accenting the fish. The bean sprouts are good, but the water spinach is better—if you can handle the chili. (Try pairing it with the fresh, cold papaya salad.) The restaurant is small with a generic ethnic interior, but the food and exceptional service more than make up for any deficiencies in décor.
Thai menu. Lunch, dinner. $

Salt

1/F, 9 Trio Building, Jiangtaixi Lu, Chaoyang District, 010-6437-8457; www.saltrestaurantbeijing.com
Opened by the same owner as the ever-popular Brazilian restaurant Alameda and housed in the Trio complex with other Western restaurants and nightclubs, Salt has a sleek and stylish interior and foreigner-friendly vibe. The international menu features everything from steak to duck to cod. The prix fixe menu is in English and offers a choice of two or three courses. Save room for dessert, particularly the chocolate soufflé with a white chocolate center. Sit at the bar for an entertaining view of the open kitchen.
International menu. Lunch, dinner. Tuesday-Saturday; Sunday brunch. Closed Monday. $$$

Serve the People

1 Xiwu Jie (opposite Spanish embassy), Sanlitun, Chaoyang
District, 010-8454-4580
This perennially packed Thai restaurant is housed in a small space, but the décor is pleasing to the eye. The pad thai, grilled beef salad and curries are popular, and most dishes are authentic—it's often hailed as one of the best Thai restaurants in the capital.
Thai menu. Lunch, dinner. $

Sorabol

2/F, Liangmahe Building, 8 Dongsanhuan Bei Lu, Chaoyang District, 010-6590-0630;
2/F, Kempinski Hotel, Lufthansa Center, 010-6465-3388; www.kempinski-beijing.com
This popular, high-end Korean restaurant has authentic barbecue, with its kalbi being the best, whether you order it marinated or not. The food comes beautifully arranged, and those who order the Korean barley will find that their tea cups are never empty. Menu standouts include kimchee and stone pot bimbimbap.
Korean menu. Lunch, dinner. $

South Beauty

3/F Pacific Century Place, Gongti Bei Lu, Chaoyang District, 010-6539-3502;
L220, 2/F, China World Trade Center (west wing), 1 Jianguomenwai Dajie, Chaoyang District, 010-6505-0809;
68 Anli Lu, Sunshine Plaza (east gate), Asian Games Village,

Traditional Chinese tea

Chaoyang District, 010-6495-1201; 19-24 Ground Floor, Henderson Centre, Jianguomennei Dajie, Dongcheng District, 010-6518-7603; North B1, Kerry Centre Mall, Chaoyang District, 010-8529-9459 This Sichuan restaurant is popular with locals but offers a picture menu to clue in visitors to the vast array of spicy, flavorful dishes created by the kitchen. Lettuce in sesame sauce, mapo tofu, ribs and Sichuan cold noodles are all popular dishes.
Sichuan menu. Lunch, dinner. $

South Silk Road (Cha Ma Gu Dao)

3/F, Building D, SOHO New Town, 88 Jianguo Lu, Chaoyang District, 010-8580-4286; 12-13, 19A Shichahai Qianhai Xiyan, Xicheng District, 010-6615-5515;

2-3/F, North Building 4, Area 2, Anhuili, Chaoyang District, 010-6481-3261 With its high ceilings and funky, industrial feel, it's no wonder that this Yunnan cuisine restaurant was opened by an artist. The delicious fare includes rice noodles dunked in piping-hot broth tableside (guoqiao mixian); smoked sausage; and fresh, raw fish, also put in boiling hot broth at the table (guoqiao yu).
Yunnan menu. Lunch, dinner. $

Suboksung (Shou Fu Cheng)

1/F, Hyundai Building B, 38 Xiaoyun Lu, Chaoyang District, 010-8453-9999 Tucked deep in the basement of the Microsoft building and the Hyundai Motor Tower, this Korean restaurant is usually filled with hungry workers from the surrounding office towers. The reasonably

PHOTO: COURTESY SHANGRA-LA HOTEL

雪水烹茶天臺味

LL-JACKSON

The Orchard

priced dishes are satisfying, and the side dishes are especially good (and you can ask for more, free of charge). Complimentary barley tea and fruit are provided to clean your palate. The stone pot bimbimbap is superb, and the barbecue satisfying. The restaurant does not aim to impress with its interior, which is average, but the food makes up what the décor lacks. *Korean menu. Dinner. $$*

Three Guizhou Men

6 Guanghua Xi Lu, Chaoyang District, 010-6502-1733; 1/2/F, Building 7, 1011 Jianwai SOHO, 39 Dongsanhuan (East Third Ring Road), Chaoyang District, 010-5869-0598; 2/F, 8 Gongti Xi Lu, Chaoyang District, 010-6551-8517

Opened by three artists from Guizhou (naturally), who were originally looking for another way to supplement their incomes while they practiced their crafts, this restaurant has a hip vibe that reflects the roots of its owners. The cuisine has been adjusted with less oil and spiciness to suit Beijingers' tastes, but the sour fish soup (suantangyu) and the peppermint salad (xiangban bohe) are still flavorful and authentic. If you're feeling adventurous, try the famously spicy Guizhou pickled vegetables. The rice bean curd, lavender tea with milk, and mango-and-ice purée are also favorites. Though only a few years old, the popularity of the original has helped spawn several locations across the city. *Guizhou menu. Lunch, dinner. $$*

Wish Restaurant & Lounge Bar

6 Fangyuan Xili, Lido Garden, Chaoyang District, 010-6438-1118/8883; www.wutong-wish.com

This open, airy space is enclosed with huge windows, making for a relaxing, inviting atmosphere in which to enjoy tasty fusion dishes, which are essentially Chinese but served with Western considerations. Sample the fresh walnut salad, cod in pumpkin soup or eggplant-bacon rolls. The restaurant targets a posh expat crowd, but prices remain modestly in check. The many teas, desserts and appetizer-sized portions mean it's also a good spot to unwind during the day or at night with a glass of wine. *Chinese menu. Lunch, dinner. $$*

Xinjiang Red Rose Restaurant

7 Xiang Xingfu Yicun, Sanlitun (opposite the north gate of Worker's Stadium), Chaoyang District, 010-6415-5741

You can't go wrong at this Xinjiang restaurant if you stick to the simple dishes that are the hallmark of the northwestern China region, including lamb kebabs, chicken with handmade noodles and veg-

etables (dapanji), roast goat, or Xinjiang stir-fried noodles (latiaozi). A Red Rose experience comes complete with loud music and dancing girls, which keep tourists streaming in year after year. *Xinjiang menu. Lunch, dinner. $*

Dongcheng District
Afunti

2A Houguaibang Hutong, Chaoyangmennei Dajie, Dongcheng District, 010-6527-2288/6525-1071

This Xinjiang-style restaurant might look like a tourist trap, with its campy dance performances and live entertainment, but knowing what to order—for example, chicken with noodles and vegetables (dapanji), sesame mutton, and lemon beef—makes the theatricals feel charming rather than trite. Though the food is pricey, it will be worth it when you see your fellow diners dancing on the tables. *Xinjiang menu. Lunch, dinner. $*

Crystal Jade

L404, 4/F, Building A, The Place, 9 Guanghua Lu, 010-6587-1228; BB78-BB82, Oriental Plaza, 1 Dongchangan Jie, Dongcheng District, 010-8515-0238; 6/F, Shin Kong Place, 87 Jianguo Lu, 010-6533-1150

Crystal Jade serves exquisite dim sum in an elegant setting complete with mirrored walls and chandeliers. The white radish cakes are perfect and not too greasy. The Cantonese roasted meats, such as the barbecue pork and roast chicken, are also standouts. Those with deep pockets should opt for the lobster, abalone or the sought-after and rare shark's fin.

Pan-Asian menu. Lunch, dinner. $

Ding Ding Xiang

1/F, 14 Dongzhong Jie, Dongzhimenwai, Dongcheng District, 010-6417-2546; 2/F, Yuanjia International Apartments, 40 Dongzhong Jie, Dongzhimenwai, Dongcheng District, 010-6417-9289; 6F, Shin Kong Place, 87 Jianguo Lu, Chaoyang District, 010-6530-5997/7172

Ding Ding Xiang, with its sleek, stylish, contemporary décor, is a modern alternative to the noisy, steam-filled rooms of typical family-style hot pot restaurants, where you cook your own food in a pot filled with your choice of bubbling sauce. The signature paste-like sesame dipping sauce is popular, as is the shaobing, a chewy bread coated with sesame seeds that's crispy on the outside. For vegetarians, there's a mushroom-based broth.

Hot pot menu. Lunch, dinner. $

Dong Lai Shun

198 Wangfujing Dajie, Dongcheng District, 010-6513-9661; 5/F, Sun Dong An Plaza, 138 Wangfujing Dajie, Dongcheng District, 010-6528-0932; 5/F, Chengxiang Business Center, 23A Fuxing Lu, Haidian District, 010-6829-6775; 31 Huawei Bei Li, Chaoyang District, 010-6778-1952

Made in China

Cepe

This classic Mongolian hot pot eatery has franchises across the country, with dozens in Beijing alone. The mutton hot pot, or self-cooked, boiled slices of mutton and other raw vegetables, is a recipe that dates back to the Yuan Dynasty. (Legend has it that Genghis Khan created the dish by quickly slaughtering some lamb, dipping the pieces in boiling water and eating it immediately to gain strength and warmth to lead his troops into battle.) The heartiness of the concoction makes it a Beijing winter favorite.
Hot pot menu. Dinner. $

Lei Garden

3/F, Jingbao Dasha (Tower),

89 Jingbao Jie, Dongcheng District, 010-8522-1212
Lei Garden serves traditional and exquisitely prepared Cantonese dishes in a simple but classy environment. Local celebrities and politicians are often found dining here. The sea salt–steamed chicken, which is steamed for eight hours with salt sourced in Fukien, has a perfectly crispy skin and a juicy interior. The Kunming duck is another signature dish, as are many of the traditional Asian desserts, including mango pudding.
Cantonese menu. Dinner. $

Made in China

1/F Grand Hyatt Hotel, 1A Dongchangan Jie, Dongcheng District, 010-8518-1234
This restaurant, tucked inside the sprawling Grand Hyatt hotel, boasts a superb version of traditional Peking duck, but don't overlook the other northern Chinese dishes on the menu, such as beggar's chicken or pork-and-leek dumplings. The upscale interior reflects a blend of old-world and modern-day China, and the extensive wine list is something that less fancy duck restaurants might not offer. Other star dishes include sesame spinach and bean curd and ground-beef noodles.
Beijing menu. Breakfast, lunch, dinner. $$

Red Capital Club

*66 Dongsi Jiutiao, Dongcheng
District, 010 8401-6152/8886;
www.redcapitalclub.com.cn*

This courtyard restaurant, which is sister to the boutique hotel Red Capital Residence a few doors down, relies heavily on Maoist kitsch, from the menu made up of favored Communist party dishes to the '50s-era lounge (there's even a telephone with a recording of Mao speaking on the other end). Menu creations have fanciful names like "south of clouds" (fish baked in a bamboo basket) or "behind silken fans" (artfully arranged steamed asparagus). Prices are high and the experience is aimed firmly at tourists, but a meal here is a unique peek into 1950s Beijing.

Chinese menu. Dinner. Reservations recommended. $$$

Tiandi Yijia

*140 Nanchizi Dajie, Dongcheng
District, 010-8511-5556*

This restaurant serves imperial Chinese cuisine in a regal setting. High-backed, wooden Ming dynasty chairs surround long tables under a glass ceiling, and other antiques dot the room. A pond with koi adds to the quiet, elegant atmosphere. Signature dishes include foie gras, abalone, shark's fin soup, cod and Kobe beef.

Chinese menu. Lunch, dinner. $

Haidian District

Blu Lobster

*29 Zizhuyuan Lu, Shangri-
La Hotel—Beijing, Haidian
District, 010-6841-2211;
www.shangri-la.com*

This restaurant tucked inside the Shangri-La Hotel shimmers with its huge glass chandeliers and azure accents. The food is creative and inventive, and the beautifully presented dishes and top-notch service provide a well-rounded dining experience. Popular items include the lobster bisque and lobster dishes, but go for the tasting menu to sample the Irish-born chef's signature creativity and intricately arranged food. Plan plenty of time for a leisurely visit so you can have an after-dinner peak at the hotel's gorgeous gardens.

Seafood menu. Dinner. $$$$

Chaishi Fengwei Zhai

*21 Ganjiakou (near Sanlihe Dong Lu),
Haidian District, 010-8838-5108*

This old-school restaurant uses a secret recipe for stewing beef in a sauce (xiaowan niurou) that keeps patrons coming back for more. Pair it with noodles and cabbage for a simple but satisfying Chinese meal. The restaurant isn't easy to find, but it's worth persevering to experience the straightforward, authentic cooking.

Beijing menu. Lunch, dinner $

Blu Lobster

Xicheng District
Cepe

Lobby level, The Ritz-Carlton Beijing—Financial Street, 1 Jin Cheng Fang East, Xicheng District, 010-6601-6666; www.ritzcarlton.com
The Italian dishes served at this upscale eatery are as colorful as the leather chairs and contemporary artwork that decorate the streamlined space. Cepe is Italian for mushrooms, which are found in many dishes, including the ricotta-stuffed, roasted eggplant appetizer. Be sure to ask for a pairing from the wide selection of Italian wines, and save room for dessert classics like tiramisu.
Italian menu. Lunch, dinner. $$$$

SUBU

4/F, Seasons Place Shopping Center, 2 Jinchengfang Jie, Xicheng District, 010-6622-0261/0211
Housed in the sparkling (and often deserted) Seasons Place mall in the Financial Street area, this futuristic fusion restaurant is heavy on style, courtesy of hot-shot Danish designer Johannes Torpe. Space-age-white dining pods provide a perch from which to sample dishes with influences from around Asia, from scallops in sweet-and-sour sauce to sliced beef in Sichuan peppers. There's also an extensive maki and sashimi selection, and the set lunch menu or afternoon tea offer a more inexpensive way to take in the stunning décor of this eatery.
Contemporary Asian menu. Lunch, dinner, afternoon tea. $$

Xuanwu District
Bodhi-Sake

10-16 Heiyaochang Jie, Xuanwu

PHOTO: COURTESY BLU LOBSTER

District, 010-6355-7348/6354-6155

Housed in a former ancient Buddhist temple and nunnery, Bodhi-Sake appropriately serves a wide variety of vegetarian dishes, including spicy tea tree mushrooms with celery. The formal worshipping hall has been preserved and is open to curious visitors.

Vegetarian menu. Lunch, dinner. $

Chongwen District
Li Qun

11 Beixiangfeng Hutong (south end of Zhengyi Lu Nankou), East Qianmen, Chongwen District, 010-6702-5681/6705-5578

Located in a hutong on the city's south side, this small, family-run duck joint isn't the easiest place to find, but it's popular among expats and locals who find the duck here fresher and crispier-tasting than at its competitors. In fact, some consider it the best duck in Beijing. The experience is no-frills, with humble décor and the raucousness typical of most Chinese restaurants. Reservations are recommended so that the staff can begin preparing your duck an hour before your arrival.

Beijing menu. Lunch, dinner. $

Quanjude

32 Qianmen Dajie, Chongwen District, 010-6701-1379;
14 Qianmen Xi Dajie, Xuanwu District, 010-6511-2418;

9 Shuaifuyuan Hutong, Wanfujing Dajie, Dongcheng District, 010-6525-3310;
1/F Jingxin Dasha (Tower), 2A Dongsanhuan Bei Lu, Chaoyang District, 010-6466-0896

Don't expect fireworks at this basic Peking duck restaurant chain, which has a number of branches across the city. The duck is reliably tasty and inexpensive, if somewhat fattier than other offerings. One of the oldest Peking duck restaurants in the city, Quanjude's many locations make it akin to the McDonald's of Peking duck—consistent and satisfying.

Beijing menu. Lunch, dinner. $

Shunyi District
The Orchard

Shunyi, Hegezhuang Village, Cuigezhuang Township (behind the Beijing Riviera and Quanfa Gardens), Shunyi District, 139-1121-1965/6433-6270

This suburban restaurant draws raves as much for its food as its peaceful setting among orchards and gardens. Organic ingredients and herbs are used in the creative international dishes whenever possible. The Sunday brunch is especially popular with local expats, and the restaurant's store provides more reasons to visit in the form of organic sauces, soaps, and other goodies like clothes and jewelry.

International menu. Lunch, dinner, Sunday brunch. $$

SHOPPING

PHOTO: MICHAEL BONACCI

WHERE TO **SHOP**

Chaoyang District
3.3 Shopping Center
33 Sanlitun Beijie, Chaoyang District, 010-6417-3333; www.3d3.cn

With five stories and more than 300 stores, most of which are trendy boutiques, this shopping center is popular among the younger set. It also has more affordable stores like Copa, a local line of hip clothing similar to H&M. The fifth floor houses a number of tailors, many of whom carry fabrics and guarantee a fast turnaround.
Daily, 11 a.m.–11 p.m.

Alien Street Market (Lao Fan Jie)
Yabao Lu (south of Fullink Plaza), Chaoyang District, 010-8561-4641

This recently cleaned-up market sells mostly to Russian traders, which means larger clothing and shoe sizes (and vendors greeting you in Russian). A large variety of typical flea

PURE **LUSTER**

YOU'LL BE HARD PRESSED to avoid finding a pearl market in China. The country dominates the global production of freshwater pearls. Freshwater (as opposed to saltwater) pearls form in various species of mussels and are classified in three varieties: natural, cultured and imitation.

Natural pearls are very rare and usually appear only as vintage items; you're not likely to find one in any of China's wholesale markets. Cultured pearls are much more common. While their name indicates that human pearl farmers intervened in the process by inserting a nucleus into the mussel or oyster, such pearls are not artificial. The farming method simply ensures a larger, more evenly shaped pearl that can be produced in a shorter period of time.

Imitation pearls are usually easy to spot because they look flawless and are lighter than the real thing. To see if a pearl is fake, rub it against the edge of your front teeth. If it's real, it will feel slightly gritty or sandy due to its crystalline structure, whereas a fake pearl will feel smooth. Don't be shy about doing this—it's actually a common test (just be sure to ask first).

Freshwater pearls naturally occur in a wide range of colors: white, pink, bronze, lavender, blue and green to name just a few. While white is the most common color, the most valuable colors are pastels in the pink and purple range. As a general pricing guideline, the larger the pearl, the more expensive it is. Also, the fewer blemishes, such as nicks, cracks or discoloration, the higher the quality. Spherelike round pearls are the most expensive; pearls with some symmetry, but not spherical, are next in value. Before purchasing anything, be sure to inspect each pearl for luster. Lustrous pearls have a shiny surface and provide strong, crisp reflections. Avoid pearls that appear dull or cloudy. And no matter the size or quality, be ready to bargain. Most wholesale market vendors start with high prices and anticipate lowering them.

Hongqiao Market (Pearl Market)

PHOTO: KINABALOO.COM

Colorful toys for sale

market fare can be found here, but the market is best known for its coats, pants and belts, as well as other accessories. *Daily, 9:30 a.m.–7 p.m.*

Bainaohui Computer Mall

10 Chaoyangmenwai Dajie, Chaoyang District, 010-6599-5912
This building is chock-full of everything technology-related, from PCs and laptops to flash drives and blank CDs. Whether it's software or an external hard drive you need, you'll find it here. Laptop accessories, like computer bags and sleeves, can be bought at great prices if you know how to bargain, and these are safer

purchases than the electronics, which may have warranties that are only valid in China, or computers, which may have Chinese-language software. *Daily, 9 a.m.–8 p.m.*

China World Trade Center (Guomao)

1 Jianguomenwai Dajie, Chaoyang District, 010-6505-2288; www.cwtc.com/english/about/index.asp
With 200 stores over four levels, this mall houses many high-end stores like Fendi, Celine and Hermès, as well as midrange stores like Armani Exchange and Nine West, though prices tend to be higher

here than in the United States. Besides the variety of stores and its central location, the large ice skating rink located in the basement is a big draw.
Daily, 10 a.m.–9:30 p.m.

Panjiayuan Antique Market (Dirt Market)

Panjiayuan Qiao (east of Longtan Park), Chaoyang District, 010-6775-2405
With more than 3,000 stalls, Panjiayuan has loads of goods though it's most famous for its antiques and arts and crafts. Vendors come from all over the country and sell everything from collectibles to paintings, pots to brushes, and much more. Arrive as early as 5 a.m. on the weekends for the best selection. The ethnic section is great for souvenirs like Chinese fabrics, clothes and jewelry. If you know your antiques, you just may strike gold; if not, you might find yourself pushed into buying something that's not genuine. The trick is to buy what you like and be happy with the price you pay for it. As with all flea markets, bargaining is crucial. No matter how special the wooden Buddhist statues, pottery or Mao memorabilia may look, they're not worth the original asking price.
Monday-Friday 8:30 a.m.–6 p.m., Saturday-Sunday 4:30 a.m.–6 p.m.

SHOP **SMART**

A common misconception of first-time visitors to China is that everything is inexpensive. This isn't necessarily true. Malls like Oriental Plaza, Shin Kong and Seasons Place have famous European and American name-brand retailers whose products will be at least 15–20 percent higher than the same product in the United States. This is due to China's taxes and duty on imported goods. It's definitely worth visiting these malls to witness the country's new economy in action, but you should save your shopping budget for some of China's unique and local offerings.

Knock it off

Is that a real Prada bag? Unfortunately, no. In the large markets like Silk Street or Hongqiao (Pearl Market), any well-known brands you'll encounter are likely to be knock-offs. If you think it looks too good to be a fake, then congratulations, you've discovered a really good fake. "Name-brand" ski parkas have seemingly beautiful construction with branded zippers, trim, labels and even tags. You may be tempted to purchase one, especially since the real deal in the United States costs about $300 and here they're only $25. But the old saying applies: You get what you pay for. The fake may be warm enough, but the material doesn't have the waterproof breathability of the real thing. You'll also see replicas of watches, and some will even seem like good ones with self-winding movements. While you can get one of these disposable beauties for under $20, it will be evident in a few months why you can't get automatic watches in the United States for less than $200.

How to haggle

The rule of thumb in the markets has always been to start your offer at about a quarter to a third of the price you're quoted. This doesn't really work today, as many vendors have figured this out and throw out ridiculously high prices. The new rule of thumb is to take the price that you think the item is worth, divide that by two, then bargain back up. Seems simple enough, but it's not always easy to figure out the value of things here. Some things look more expensive than they really are, and vendors are happy to take advantage of that.

Logic assumes that handcrafts and paintings would be at least a few dollars multiplied by the amount of time it takes to produce them. What's difficult for many Western visitors to comprehend is that the minimum wage in China is around RMB5 per hour, which is about $0.50 at current exchange rates. The time it takes to create these items is also less than you would assume, because the artist has usually been doing it repeatedly for many years. Articles of clothing are produced at alarming speed and contain less than $1 of labor. For knockoff items, no research and development or quality assurance costs go into them. In most cases, only the cost of materials matters. Considering that the materials are usually relatively low quality and purchased at bulk prices, you can imagine why a coat would have enough margin for the manufacturer, distributor and vendor to be happy with a $15 "street price." Basic cotton T-shirts with various designs and logos should cost you no more than RMB10, while nice shirts and sweaters should cost RMB35 to RMB75. Don't let the design or the false brand fool you into thinking one item is more expensive than another. At the end of the day, these items are commodities that could be priced by their material quality multiplied by weight.

Silk Street Market

8 Xiushui Dongjie, Jianguomenwai Dajie, Chaoyang District, 010-5169-8800
The ambience isn't the same since this market, known for its knock-offs, was moved from its original alleyways to a modern, six-story building in Chaoyang, but it's still the city's best bet for luggage, handbags, clothing or souvenirs. Most vendors speak some English, so Chinese language skills aren't required to negotiate—just be prepared to drive a hard bargain. Look hard at the quality of the item you're buying, especially the designer knock-offs. There are good deals on accessories like scarves and gloves, as well as T-shirts and traditional clothes.
Daily, 9 a.m.–9 p.m.

Shin Kong Place

87 Jianguo Lu, Chaoyang District, 010-6530-5888; www.shinkong-place.com
Currently the newest (and some say the best) shopping mall in Beijing, Shin Kong Place has everything in one spot—top-notch restaurants, a food court, clothing and accessories of all brands, a bookstore and cafés. It's also connected to China Central

Skating inside at China World
Trade Center

Place and adjacent to the new Ritz-Carlton. On the first floor, a high-tech, complimentary locker system is available to store coats or jackets you don't feel like toting (but not valuables). Trek the floors of the Japanese-style department store to find an array of brands, whether Chinese or European, or venture out into the mall for Marc Jacobs, Gucci or Shiatzy Chen, but remember that prices of Western brands tend to be higher than at home. When you get tired, head upstairs to one of a number of restaurants that are better than your usual mall fare, like Ding Ding Xiang or Din Tai Fung. Grab authentic French pastries at Fauchon. *Daily, 10 a.m.–10 p.m.*

Chongwen District
Hongqiao Market (Pearl Market)

Tiantan Dong Lu (east of the Temple of Heaven), Chongwen District, 010-6713-3354

You can find almost anything in Hongqiao with its rows and rows of vendors, but it's most notable for its pearl market, where Tony Blair and Bill Clinton are said to have shopped. Stalls of vendors display their many strands of pearls, most of which are freshwater. Locals do shop here, but the market's status as a tourist attraction means that

PHOTO: KINABALOO.COM

BUYING
JADE

Jade has been a part of Chinese culture since its beginning, as early as 5000 B.C., and it is one of the country's most cherished stones. Jade is a tough mineral that resists chipping and breaking. It is often classified as either soft jade (nephrite) or hard jade (jadeite).

Nephrite jade is found in fewer colors than jadeite. Instead of a bright emerald green, nephrite is often a grayish or mottled green. Also, because it is softer than jadeite, finished pieces cannot be as highly polished. Until jadeite was imported from Burma (Myanmar) in the 1700s, China only had access to nephrite, making jadeite scarcer and more valuable, as it still is today.

Jadeite comes in many colors, including green, white, lavender, yellow, orange, black and red. Evenly colored, translucent, emerald-green jadeite is called Imperial Jade; it's very rare and very expensive.

When purchasing the stone, look for pieces with uniform color

Jade trinkets

throughout, although multicolor pieces with distinctive patterns are also popular. Intense colors of jade are most desirable, carrying a higher price tag, and green is the most popular color of jade, closely followed by lavender. Keep in mind that semi-transparent to translucent jade is more valuable than opaque jade. Avoid stones with many cracks or other visible flaws. Dishonest dealers often try to pass off dyed quartz and other stones as jade, so examine your piece carefully before purchasing it.

bargaining is essential to avoid overpaying. Beware of purchasing "name–brand" electronics— they might be counterfeit. You can also get traditional Chinese clothing, fans, tablecloths and other gifts to bring home.
Daily, 8:30 a.m.–7 p.m.

Dongcheng District
The Malls at Oriental Plaza
1 Dongchangan Jie, Dongcheng District, 010-8518-8888; www.orientalplaza.com
Connected to the Grand Hyatt, this shopping paradise is large enough to be divided into six sections, each housing different types of stores and entertainment. It has a movie theater, one of the largest CD/DVD stores in the city, high-end Chinese shops like Shanghaixu and Shanghai Tang, and other international brands like La Perla, Nina Ricci, Swarovski and Burberry. After shopping, dine at a restaurant such as Crystal Jade or take a quick break and hop into the Yoshinoya (which is better than its U.S. counterparts) or Starbucks. There's also Mr. Pizza, Dairy Queen and Japanese cream puff chain Beard Papa's.
Daily, 9:30 a.m.–10 p.m.

Xicheng District
Joy City
131 Xidan Bei Dajie, Xicheng District, 010-6612-9999

The latest addition to Xidan, which is already a shopping haven and a favorite hangout for young Beijingers, will no doubt attract even more people to the area. Targeting an upscale clientele, the new 13-story mall, houses a cinema with 13 screens and supposedly the world's longest escalator. It is also home to the second Beijing locations of Zara and Uniqlo, the Japanese superstore similar to Gap.

Seasons Place Shopping Center
2 Jinchengfang Jie, Fuxingmen, Xicheng District, 010-6622-0888, 800-810-0881; www.seasonsplace.com
Despite being connected to the stylish Ritz-Carlton— Financial Street in the booming business district, this shopping center is often quiet. Still, this is where you can find Gucci, Dior and Chloé. The center also houses the only Lane Crawford in the city, a popular Hong Kong–based chain that sells high-end designer labels in a chic atmosphere. The basement level features a well-stocked grocery that stocks everything from wine to produce to chocolates.
Daily, 10 a.m.–9 p.m.

798

ART DISTRICT

THIS CUTTING-EDGE COMMUNITY IS THE PLACE TO BROWSE ART AND FASHION, AND SOAK UP CULTURE

THE DASHANZI ART DISTRICT was originally home to the 798 Factory, which produced electronics. When the factory closed, the low-rent, Bauhaus-style space, which today provides plenty of space and light for its exhibitions, drew artists from all over the world to open studios and galleries. Today, this former industrial area houses a trendy, avant-garde art community of galleries, art centers, bars, restaurants, coffee shops, studios and design companies. You'll find all kinds of art here, from prints and sculptures to paintings and books. The district is also synonymous with events and new product releases—brands like Christian Dior, Nike and Paul Smith hold fashion shows here.

Taxis drop visitors at the front gate, and from there it takes a stroll into the heart of the complex before you'll spy many signs directing you to the dozens of different galleries. Beijing Tokyo Art Projects is an acclaimed spot for hip installations, while Star Gallery, White Space and Beijing Commune all have constantly changing exhibits. For fashion-influenced and contemporary fine art photography, stop in at Paris-Beijing Photo Gallery. Perennial favorite 798 Photo has unique Mao-era pictures and posters plus changing avant-garde exhibits. Next door is a sprawling area with everything from paintings to multimedia installations. Red Gate Gallery has several other locations, but the 798 Space is a good spot for browsing this trend-setting contemporary art source.

If all this browsing leaves you longing for a cup of coffee or a sandwich, try At Café for creamy cappuccinos and a lunch menu that changes daily. When you're ready for a full meal, the Old Factory bar, which still has the original electronics machines in place, serves up great Italian cuisine. For late-night lounging, go to Cave Café, which stays open after the galleries close.

798 Art District

4 Jiuxian Qiao Lu (Dashanzi Art District), Chaoyang District, 010-6437-6248/6438-4862; www.798space.com Galleries daily, 10:30 to 6-7:30 p.m.

BEIJING

Ritz-Carlton Spa Fitness and Salon

SPAS

Western-style spas used to be hard to find in Beijing. Other than no-frills massage and reflexology parlors (which sound, and often are, pretty sketchy), pampering spots were rare. But with the scores of new international luxury hotels came plenty of sparkling, sprawling spas. Now you can have the kind of experience you'd find in Thailand or Indonesia but with a local twist. Many spas are fusing modern therapies with ancient Chinese medicine, giving travelers a reason (besides all the pollution and crazy congestion) to book a treatment or two while here.

Hotel Spas
Chi Spa

Shangri-La Hotel, 29 Zizhuyuan Lu, Xicheng District, 010-6841-2211; www.shangri-la.com

This mystic spa is sure to help you find your chi (the force that governs your well-being and vitality). The modern interpretation of a Tibetan temple stimulates the senses with incense and the sound of singing bowls (a type of bell). Signature treatments include the Chi Balance, a blend of acupressure and both energizing and relaxing massage with oils to suit your yin/yang; and the Aroma Vitality, a combination of Swedish, shiatsu and reflexology massages. Or sign up for one of the "journeys." The Enchanted Journey, for example, includes a Himalayan bath therapy, Tsampa rub (a barley scrub) and massage.

Club Oasis Fitness Center and Spa

Grand Hyatt Beijing, 1 Dongchangan Jie, Dongcheng District, 010-8518-1234; www.beijing.grand.hyatt.com

This clean, contemporary spa with Asian accents offers traditional Chinese massage and reflexology, manicures and pedicures, and more. But perhaps the highlight is the sprawling, basement-level indoor pool whose landscaping combines palm trees, star-studded skies and waterfalls.

Heavenly Spa by Westin

Westin Beijing—Financial Street, 9B Jinrong Jie, Xicheng District, 010-6629-7878; www.westin.com

With its pretty, Zen waiting room and huge spa suites, this is the perfect spot to escape for a few hours. Try the Chinese massage, in which nerve centers are stimulated with acupressure. The Pearl White facial uses active ingredients from pearls to reduce dark spots and brighten skin. When you're done being rubbed and exfoliated, you can soak in an infinity bath or splash around in the rain forest shower.

LeSpa

Sofitel Wanda Beijing, 93 Jianguo Lu, Tower C Wanda Plaza, Chaoyang District, 010-8599-6666; www.sofitel.com

This luxurious spa features several Chinese ancestral traditions. The Jiangsu Serenity treatment, inspired by the area at the mouth of the Yangtze and Fuchun rivers in China, begins with a foot bath followed by a massage that delves into pressure points on your head, shoulder and neck to drive out every bit of tension. There are also warm ginger scrubs, stimulating massages and pampering beauty treatments for hands and feet, as well as Lancôme cabins, which offer a multisensory experience.

Bodhi Sense Spa

The Ritz-Carlton Spa, Fitness and Salon

Ritz Carlton Beijing—Financial Street, 1 Jinchengfang Dongjie, Xicheng District, 010-6601-6666; www.ritzcarlton.com

This spa occupies an entire floor of the hotel and includes 11 treatment rooms and two relaxation lounges. The staff recently added several Balinese treatments, including the Boreh, where you're scrubbed down with ground spices and then wrapped in a warm blanket before being slathered with a cooling cucumber body conditioner. The signature massage combines acupressure and aromatherapy to loosen up your muscles. Heated herbs are then applied on the meridian points (connected points that affect a specific organ or other part of your body) to ease muscle tension and soothe nerves. Once you're nice and relaxed, lounge by the mosaic-tiled pool and watch a movie—the dimly lit area has a big screen on one end on which the staff plays classic films.

The Ritz-Carlton Spa, The Ritz-Carlton Beijing

83A Jianguo Lu, Chaoyang District, 010-5908-8888; www.ritzcarlton.com

Choose from a number of fantastic treatments that promise to leave you scrubbed, rubbed, oiled—and stress-free. The Ritz Fusion begins with a foot ritual and is followed by a blend of Oriental herbs applied to those handy meridian points to wipe away your tension and make you feel oh-so-relaxed.

PHOTO: COURTESY BODHI SENSE SPA

St. Regis Spa

St. Regis Hotel Beijing,
21 Jianguomenwai Dajie,
Chaoyang District, 010-6460-
6688; www.stregis.com

More than 40 Western and Eastern treatments are offered at this spa, from a massage that promises to restore regular sleep patterns after a long flight to herbal scrubs that will stimulate blocked channels. The Beijing Body Renewal promises to help you recover from all the city dust and dirt and includes a full-body hot-oil wrap, head and scalp acupressure massage, and hand and foot treatments. The glass-enclosed pool is nice for a swim. The spa uses water from a natural hot spring 1,400 meters below the hotel.

Serenity Spa

The Regent Beijing, 99 Jinbao Jie,
Dongcheng District, 010-8522-
1888; www.regenthotels.com

The smells and sounds at this exotic spa will get you in the mood for any number of European or Chinese therapies. Try the signature treatment, which includes a body scrub, bath ritual, facial and a massage with a special blend of aromatic oils. Treatment rooms are decorated with Chinese antiques and fabrics. Every last detail is attended to (even the aromatic bowl of fresh blossoms placed under the massage table,

an unexpected and pleasant visual when you're facedown). Stop by the hair and beauty salon to leave looking as good as you feel.

Day Spas
Bodhi Sense

17 Gongti Beilu, Chaoyang
District, 010-6417-9595;
www.bodhi.com.cn

This swank spa offers many different types of massage plus facials using Dermatologica products. Try the Vitality package, which includes a peppermint foot soak, lemon foot polish, body scrub, aromatherapy bath and massage. Treatments are followed by tea.
Daily, 11 a.m. to 12:30 a.m.

Dragonfly @ the Forbidden City

60 Donghuamen Dajie, Dongcheng
District, 010-6527-9368;
www.dragonfly.net.cn

Step into this quietly luxurious, candlelit spa and feel instantly relaxed. This popular spa chain specializing in massage, particularly foot massage, is open until the wee hours.
Daily, 11 a.m. to 1 a.m.

i spa

5F, Tower 2, Taiyue Suites, 16 Nan
Sanlitun Lu, Chaoyang District, 010-
6507-1517; Napa Club, Shashun
Lu, Xiaotangshan, Changping

Ritz-Carlton Spa Fitness and Salon

District, 010-6178-7795;
www.ispa.cn

This Thai spa (not to be confused with one with a similar name at the Intercontinental Hotel) offers a wide variety of treatments, including tropical fruit scrubs, hydrating facials and the vigorous massage for which Thais are known. There are also a variety of packages, including the Phuket Homeland package, which includes aroma steaming, a fruity scrub, fresh fruit body wrap, and an aroma body massage. The new location on the outskirts of Beijing is a great escape for a night.
Daily, 11 a.m.-11 p.m.

Zenspa

Building 1, 8A Xiaowuji Lu, Chaoyang District, 010-8731-2530;
www.zenspa.com.cn

This spa is set in a traditional Chinese courtyard house. While visiting may feel like taking a step back in time, this spa is always introducing new therapies. Try the signature Asian-fusion massage, which uses various styles of Asian massage, including Chinese, Thai and Japanese. It's just the ticket for sore muscles. The antioxidant Thanaka uses an herb found in Burma to nourish skin. If you're making a day of it, the Ultimate Indulgence uses a scrub of gold leaves, imported Thai herbs and rose petals; this is followed by a honey wrap, Royal Thai

floral bath or Cleopatra milk bath, one-hour aromatherapy massage, and a Burmese Thanaka facial.
Daily (except for the first three days of Chinese New Year) 11 a.m.-11 p.m.

Natural Wonders

Chinese medicine has captured international attention for years thanks to its powers in healing all manner of ailment, from muscle aches to headaches, using natural remedies and acupuncture. If you're curious about exploring the ancient world of Chinese medicine, Beijing is the place to do it. The nation's most famous producer of natural remedies is Tongrentang, a pharmaceutical company that sells everything from medicines for soothing nerves to treatments for digestion. The company has emporiums all over the world from Hong Kong to San Francisco, but the Beijing location on Dazhalan, a pedestrian-only street in Qianmen, is worth a visit. Bring an interpreter and ask for a consultation before purchasing the right dried herbs, potions or even dried seahorses for your ailment.
24 Dazhalan, Qianmen, Chongwen District

BEIJING

Centro Bar

ON THE TOWN

NIGHT**LIFE**

Houhai

Houhai was once a peaceful, serene area next to the lake. Then the bars started popping up, in just a short few years transforming the area into a nightlife mecca. In addition to bars and restaurants, there are stores where you can buy trinkets. Although famous for its nightlife, Houhai is worthy of an all-day excursion—rent a boat and relax on the lake.

Bed Bar (or Bed Tapas & Bar)

17 Zhangwang Hutong,
Jiu Gulou Dajie, Xicheng
District, 010-8400-1554
Located in a hutong in a converted traditional courtyard house, Bed Bar has many separate rooms, providing the perfect environment for lounging or a date. The Chinese kang-style beds (more like platforms than mattresses) are ideal for relaxing, and the quieter environment is suitable for conversations. Bed is known for sangria, but its signature drink is the mojito. Tasty Western-style tapas make for good bar food.
Daily, 2 p.m.–3 a.m.

No Name Bar

3 Qianhai Dongyan (next to
Kaorouji restaurant), Xicheng
District, 010-6401-8541
This legendary bar was the first to open on Houhai and is often credited for having made the area the nightlife hub it is today. The bar originally didn't even have a sign on the door, so only those in the know would show up. The interior design changes from time to time, but the atmosphere is always mellow and perfect for enjoying a coffee or beer with a view of the lake.
Daily, Noon–2 a.m.

Sanlitun

Near Workers' Stadium, centered on
Gongti Bei Lu, Chaoyang District
This area, with its famous Bar Street, was one of Beijing's first big night spots. It's divided into three areas—north, west and central. Many of the bars are concentrated in the north and central areas. The west area, which lies right outside of Workers' Stadium, is considered separate and is home to many clubs and live music venues. The former south area has been completely demolished.

Bar Blu

4/F, Tongli Studio, Sanlitun Bei Lu,
Chaoyang District, 010-6416-7567
As at many of the bars in Sanlitun, a mostly foreign crowd gathers here to enjoy the drinks, pool tables, happy hour specials and

international DJs nightly. No matter what you prefer in a nightlife venue, whether dancing or drinking or just enjoying the crowd, Bar Blu will leave you satisfied. Enjoy the roof terrace on warm nights.
Daily, Sunday-Thursday 4 p.m.–2 a.m., Friday- Saturday 4 p.m.–4 a.m.

The Tree

43 Bei Sanlitun Nan (behind Poachers Inn, across the street from Sanlitun Hospital), Chaoyang District, 010-6415-1954; www.treebeijing.com
Though many come here for the selection of Belgian beers, the Tree is also famous for its wood-fired pizza. Wash down a four-cheese pizza with a Hoegaarden or De Koninck, which are on tap. The Tree also provides a relaxed environment for a night out on the town.
Sunday-Tuesday 10 a.m.–2 a.m., Wednesday-Thursday 10 a.m.–3 a.m., Friday-Saturday 10 a.m.–4 a.m.

Rickshaw

24H Sanlitun Nan Lu (just south of Gongti Bei Lu), Chaoyang District, 010-6500-4330; www.beijingrickshaw.com
People come to this dive bar for the chicken wings, burritos and Stella Artois on tap. The cozy, sometimes overly smoky atmosphere draws crowds, and the multiple TVs attract sports fans.

Large groups always seem to begin—or end—the night here.
Daily, 24 hours.

Q Bar

6/F, Eastern Inn Hotel, Sanlitun Nan Lu (across from Chaoyang Hospital, south of Beer Mania), Chaoyang District, 010-6595-9239; www.qbarbeijing.com
Situated on top of a somewhat nondescript hotel, Q Bar is a pleasant surprise with a dimly lit, stylishly decorated interior and a spacious rooftop with plenty of greenery. Patio furniture in the form of wooden tables, folding chairs and backed benches creates a warm, inviting atmosphere from which to sip a cocktail and take in the view of the city. The friendly bartenders make great martinis.
Daily, 6 p.m.–2 a.m.

Workers' Stadium (Gongti) Area

Built in 1959 and host to soccer matches and concerts, the Workers' Stadium has attracted crowds to the surrounding area, which has become home to some of the city's biggest and most popular nightclubs. Many bars, lounges and live music venues are located across from the North Gate in the parking lot. The stadium is only a 10–15 minute walk from the rest

Q Bar

Yugong Yishan

of the action in the Sanlitun area, so clubbing after a meal or bar hopping is an easy option.

Babi Club

8 Gongti Xi Lu, Chaoyang District, 010-6551-3338; www.babiclub.com

This Sichuan chain recently underwent construction, adding a dance floor to satisfy its patrons. You'll find all types of music here, including hip-hop, house and R&B. Newly added booths overlook the dance floor and DJ booth. There's no cover during the week.

Daily, hours vary.

Mix

Inside Worker's Stadium North Gate, Chaoyang District, 010-6530-2889/6530-2689

Located just across the street, Mix is Vics' top competitor. Loyal patrons of the latter consider Mix a knock-off of sorts, but the places are very similar—which club you prefer boils down to a matter of personal preference. Mix plays mostly hip-hop and gets top DJs from around the world.

Daily, 7:30 p.m.–6 a.m.

Nan Jie

4 Gongti Bei Lu (in the parking lot opposite the North Gate of Workers' Stadium), Chaoyang District, 010-6413-0963

Famous for its cheap drinks, Nan Jie is usually packed with young people, many of whom are students. The low cost of the drinks could be worth braving the loud crowd and the sticky, sweaty mess before journeying to your next destination.

Daily, 6 p.m.–4 a.m.

Richy

6 Gongti Xi Lu, Chaoyang District, 010-6551-9081; www.babyface.com.cn

Originally the popular Babyface, this Guangzhou-based chain was recently renovated with a fresh look and given a new name. It remains to be seen whether it will draw even larger crowds than its predecessor, but the hip-hop goes all night long, and there's only a cover charge when the big DJs are in town.

Daily, 8 p.m.–5 a.m.

Salsa Caribe

4 Gongti Bei Lu (behind The Bookworm), Chaoyang District, 010-6507-7821

Salsa Caribe is the most popular salsa club in Beijing and is widely regarded as the most authentic with its live band from Colombia and catchy salsa beats. There's also a live Cuban performance group.

Daily, 7 p.m.–2 a.m.

Q Bar

Vics

Gongti Lu (inside Workers' Stadium North Gate), 010-5293-0333
Considered one of the city's original dance clubs, Vics plays hip-hop, reggae, R&B and pop for a hip Chinese crowd. Recently remodeled, it's now one of the biggest clubs in the city. If you're looking for dancing, this is the place—just keep in mind that the club is known as something of a meat market. Wednesday nights are ladies' nights, which means no cover before midnight.
8:30 p.m.–after midnight

Other Areas
Block 8

8 Chaoyang Xi Lu, Chaoyang District, 010-6508-8585; www.block8.cn
Block 8 houses upscale restaurants Haiku and Med, iUltra Lounge, an outdoor patio called The Beach, and a rooftop terrace complete with views of the city skyline and cabanas and beds. One of the most contemporary and posh hangouts in the city, Block 8 provides a fancy night out on the town all in one place. And since it's located in the Number Eight complex on Chaoyang Xi Lu, other places to eat and hang out are within a few minutes' walk.
Med and Haiku, daily, 6 p.m.–11 p.m.; iUltra Lounge, daily, 6 p.m.–2 a.m.

PHOTO: COURTESY Q BAR

Centro Bar & Lounge

*1/F, Shangri-La's Kerry Centre
Hotel, 1 Guanghua Lu, Chaoyang
District, 010-6561-8833;
www.shangri-la.com*
Celebrities are frequently spotted at this lounge located in
the Kerry Centre Hotel, and the
nightly live jazz draws a sophisticated crowd, especially
on weekdays. Go during happy
hour for more reasonably priced
drinks—try the blue cheese
martini. Because of its location in the Chaoyang business
district, Centro is not ideal for
bar hopping but is perfect for
weekday after-work cocktails.
Daily, 24 hours

LAN

*12B Jianguomenwai Dajie,
Chaoyang District, 010-5109-
6012; www.lanbeijing.com*
Though the food (a tasty blend
of Western and Chinese) at this
Philippe Starck-designed restaurant is well worth sampling, it's
the buzzing lounge scene and
over-the-top décor that attracts
a well-dressed crowd of Beijing
hipsters and in-the-know foreigners to this lounge and restaurant.
The space includes an oyster
bar, a cigar bar and private VIP
rooms for those who prefer to
keep their socializing discreet.
Daily, 11a.m.-3 a.m.

Stone Boat Bar

*Ritan Bei Lu, lakeside (southwest
corner of Ritan Park), Chaoyang
District, 010-6501-9986*
Built like an ornate Qing-era
teahouse and shaped like
a boat, the Stone Boat Bar
seems like a blatant tourist trap, but it doesn't matter.
There's live music and decent
food, and it's perfect for enjoying a day or night on the
water in Ritan Park. In the
winter, the space is heated.
The atmosphere here is relaxed—it only becomes lively when there's an event.
10 a.m.–midnight

Live Music Venues
D-22

*242 Chengfu Lu, Wudaokou,
Haidan District, 010-6265-3177;
www.d22beijing.com*
Billing itself as a bar and a music
club, D-22 has become the place
to go to hear and watch emerging Beijing musicians and artists
and their international collaborations. Currently operating as a
nonprofit, D-22 tries to keep cover
prices low and puts those yuan
back into the place, investing in
quality equipment, for example.
Loyal patrons come for the music
in spite of mediocre drinks and a
remote, university-area location.
Tuesday-Sunday 7:30 p.m.–2 a.m.

Chinese acrobats

Yugong Yishan

3-2 Zhangzizhong Lu (west courtyard, former site of Duan Qirui Government), Dongcheng District, 010-6404-2711; www.yugongyishan.com

Commonly hailed as Beijing's number one live music venue, Yugong Yishan is named after a man in a Chinese proverb who wanted to move a mountain—and actually succeeded. After its original spot outside Workers' Stadium was demolished in 2007, Yugong Yishan moved to its current, larger location in a courtyard in the Dongcheng District. Now, in addition to good music, Yugong Yishan has an interesting exterior and interior space all to itself.

Daily, 6 p.m.–2 a.m.

Theater, Concerts and Opera

Whether it's the unique, traditional Beijing opera or contemporary Chinese theater, the capital city offers plenty of entertainment after dark. You can usually secure last-minute tickets to opera, theater or circus performances at a relatively low price ($20 for a night at the opera, for example) with the assistance of your hotel's concierge. Visit the new Opera House for a chance to experience an ancient art in a truly modern setting—the two-year-old building (a futuristic structure that looks like a massive egg) is one of Beijing's most remarkable new landmarks.

Beijing Concert Hall

1 Bei Xinhua Jie, Liubukou, Xicheng District, 010-6605-7006

The Beijing Concert Hall, constructed in 1985, was China's first professional concert hall. Home to the China National Symphony Orchestra, this is the place to go in Beijing for classical music, whether Chinese or Western. It seats more than 1,000 people and has an art exhibit space on the upper level.

Capital Theater

22 Wangfujing Dajie, Dongcheng District, 010-6524-9847

The home base of the Beijing People's Art Theater, the Capital Theater is a popular venue for watching modern Chinese theater. In a prime location, the Soviet-style building holds almost 1,000 people. Most performances are in Chinese, though sometimes international productions are staged.

Chang An Grand Theater

7 Jianguomennei Dajie, Dongcheng District, 010-6510-1309/1310; www.changantheater.com

The Chang An Grand Theater is a well-known traditional venue for Beijing Opera, and it's now one of the ritzier ones thanks to its new VIP seating with food and drink service. One of the larger Beijing Opera spaces, this theater holds 800 people. English subtitles make following the action easy.

OPERA IN BEIJING

Banned during the Cultural Revolution, traditional Beijing opera, with its colorful use of makeup and costumes, is alive and well in today's Beijing. A new, architecturally stunning opera house makes a prime spot to experience this fascinating ancient art form, which features stories that date from the 12th century. Players begin a rigorous training process as early as childhood to master the sword dances, movements and voice training (usually a nasal falsetto) required. Before you arrive in Beijing, check out the 1993 film *Farewell My Concubine*, a peek into the world of opera-training schools and life on stage.

Chaoyang Theater

36 Dongsanhuan Bei Lu, Chaoyang District, 010-6507-2421/1818; www.bjcyjc.com/english/english.asp
Plates, fans, bicycles, you name it: This theater, one of the most popular for Chinese acrobats, has them all. Check out this basic performance space in the heart of Beijing for a night of fun. (Though the shows are entertaining, they rarely draw a crowd.) The venue also stages opera performances.

China Puppet Theater

A1 Anhua Xili, Beisanhuan Lu, Chaoyang District, 010-6424-3698; www.puppetchina.com
Widely regarded as the place to go for Chinese puppet theater, not to mention the most kid-friendly venue for it, the China Puppet Theater uses shadow and hand puppets to tell traditional stories, both Chinese and Western. The theater also stages international acts, like the Moscow Puppet Theater.

Lao She Teahouse (Lao She Chaguan)

3 Qianmenxi Dajie (near Tiananmen square), 010-6303-6830; www.laosheteahouse.com
This famous teahouse, named after the Chinese writer Lao She and his famous play Teahouse, serves up quality tea and tasty Chinese snacks as well as Beijing opera. The classic décor reflects the traditional arts that can be experienced in this venue, whether Chinese crosstalk, folk music or acrobatics.

Liyuan Theater

1/F, Qianmen Jianguo Hotel, 175 Yongan Lu, Xuanwu District, 010-6301-6688; www.qianmenhotel.com/en/index.php

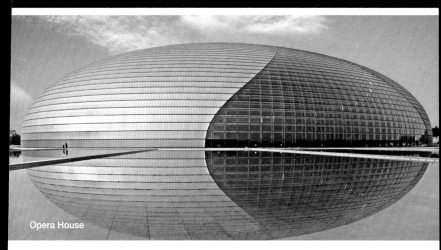
Opera House

Cosponsored by the Beijing Qianmen Jianguo Hotel and the Beijing Opera Company, the Liyuan Theater is another top venue for Beijing Opera. Whether it's watching an (interpreted) performance, buying Beijing Opera souvenirs or taking photos with actors, Liyuan guarantees a well-rounded, though perhaps touristy, Beijing opera experience.

National Center for the Performing Arts

2 Xichangan Jie, Xicheng District, 010-6655-0000; www.chncpa.org

This new, French-designed theater complex boasts a concert hall, an opera house and a theater that seats more than 1,000; the entire space is estimated to hold more than 6,000. The energy-saving silver dome is surrounded by an artificial lake. Though controversial because of its unusual modern design and its contrast with the neighborhood's character, this architectural masterpiece is worth seeing.

Mei Lanfang Grand Theater

32 Pinganli Dajie, Southeast of Guanyuan Bridge, Xicheng District, 010-6551-6590

This new theater for Beijing opera, recently constructed in hopes of reviving the traditional art form, is now the largest traditional opera venue, holding around 1,100 people. Named after one of the most famous actors in Beijing opera (Mei Lanfang, who performed in Beijing in the first half of the 20th century), the theater is located in Xidan, near Financial Street, making it one of the few venues on the west side of town.

City traffic

居然之家
JU RAN ZHI JIA
小营路
XIAO YING LU

出口
EXIT

BEIJING

AND BEYOND

PHOTO: iSTOCKPHOTO

Traditional Chinese architecture

The Great Wall

If this is your first time in Beijing, a visit to the Great Wall is a must, even if it means sneaking in a trip before a business meeting. Most likely, you'll be awake early from the time change, so you might as well take advantage of it.

Contrary to popular belief, the Great Wall is not a single continuous structure. It's a series of fortifications with a combined span of more than 4,000 miles. The sections were built between the 5th century B.C. and the 16th century by successive dynasties to protect their borders, usually from invasions from Mongolians to the north. Some sections have been restored recently and have smooth walking services, intact stairs and newly built watchtowers created to suggest the Wall's original construction. Others are little more than crumbling ruins—heart-poundingly steep, treacherous and wild. Visitors have fallen from unstable sections, and even at the restored sections, a twisted ankle is not uncommon.

The more popular sections, Badaling and Mutianyu, allow visitors to experience the Wall within half a day or less. Both are located a little more than an hour's drive from Beijing, with Badaling slightly more accessible. If you have more time and don't want to bump up against throngs of tourists or deal with lots of vendors hawking souvenirs, consider a full-day visit to the more remote sections of the wall, such as Simatai, Jiankou or Jinshanling.

Visiting the Great Wall requires at a minimum a moderate degree of mobility, with some sections being more physically challenging than others. Badaling, Mutianyu and Jinshanling offer aerial trams to take you up to scenic spots and back down.

For each of these locations, you can work with your hotel to hire a private driver, tour bus or taxi. If you use a taxi, ask the hotel to negotiate a rate with the driver to wait for you. Make sure you jot down the license plate number to identify him among other, similar-looking cars.

Badaling

Badaling is the most popular section of the wall since it's closest to Beijing. This is the section most tour companies visit, and a number of vendors here will happily exchange your RMB for their overpriced souvenirs. Beat the crowds by arriving just before 7 a.m. Take the aerial tram to the top and walk back down to the parking areas. (Note: A section of Badaling requires a challenging descent on a precipitous set of stairs.) You can check out the boutique hotel Commune by the Great Wall on your return trip—it's a recently opened, architecturally hailed complex of cutting-edge houses designed for adventurous travelers.

Jiankou

Jiankou, a scenic drive up the mountains west of Mutianyu, is considered the most dangerous section of the Wall. The mountains are steep, and it's in need of renovation. It's also pretty remote. But if you're physically fit and careful, it yields breathtaking views that make for amazing photos.

Mutianyu

If you don't mind a little extra driving time, Mutianyu is very accessible and less crowded than Badaling, and it provides a bit more of the Wall to explore. As at Badaling, you can take a tram to the top and walk back down. While there are no severe descents, there is a bit more uphill climbing. Be sure to pace yourself to make it easier and more enjoyable. You can take a kitschy alpine slide back down to the village, but keep in mind that a design flaw of the slide was solved by placing employees along the track who tell people to slow down.

Simitai and Jinshanling

Unlike Badaling and Mutianyu, the section of wall between Simatai and Jinshanling has not been restored. Since it's relatively remote, it has fewer visitors. Still, this is one of the most breathtaking sections of the wall with high vistas and sheer drop-offs on both sides. If you are physically fit and have extra time, you can trek 7.5 miles between the two end points. (Be sure to coordinate transportation for your way back.) Some areas along the route may appear isolated, but you won't be far from vendors who can provide refreshments and snacks.

The Commune by the Great Wall

Designed by Asian architects, this complex will inspire and amaze. Although the Commune is managed as an upscale hotel, nonguests are invited to tour any of the currently unoccupied homes. Located on the road between Badaling and Beijing, the Commune is easily accessible on your return from the Great Wall and will give you some incredible perspective on China's past and present. Visit www.commune.com.cn/en/ for information.

Chengde, Hebei Provence

While Beijing's Summer Palace is

Great Wall

easy to check off your sightseeing list in half a day, a three-hour trip to the northeast of Beijing will put you in Chengde, where the former summer palace of the Qing Dynasty is located. The Mountain Resort of Chengde, listed as a World Heritage site, contains one of the most impressive collections of temples and imperial gardens nestled amid a lush, rolling landscape. It's accessible by train, tour bus or private car; check with your hotel for assistance.

TOURS
Cultural Excursions

The Chinese Culture Club offers classes and excursions to both well-known and obscure destinations, while providing more insights and details than the major tour operators. What's more, the person sitting next to you is probably a foreign resident, so you get a unique opportunity to hear what living in China is like. Visit www.chinesecultureclub.org/tours/beijing.php for information.

Hiking Trips

The Beijing Hikers club is very popular with expats and locals. Tours go out almost every Saturday and Sunday. You can also coordinate individual tours to a wide range of destinations. Check its Web site for upcoming tours and contact information: www.beijinghikers.com

PHOTO: ANTONIO D'ALBORE/iSTOCKPHOTO

Statue of sitting Buddah at Chengde

登机口
To Gates

PRACTICAL **MATTERS**

Visiting China

Visitors to China require a visa before embarking on a flight to the country. Contact your closest Chinese embassy or consular office (Washington, D.C., Chicago, San Francisco, Los Angeles, New York or Houston) or visit www.china-embassy.org for information. Beijing Capital International Airport has been modernized and has a new wing open for international flights. A subway line is also being built to connect the airport to the city. Until then, taxis to the city center cost between RMB60 and RMB120 and take about 40 minutes. Be sure to use only the taxis at the airport-sanctioned taxi line; avoid taxi drivers who approach you before you reach the line.

Newspapers and Magazines

Beijing's English language paper is *China Daily*, a censored, cheerful vehicle for delivering official news to expats and visiting locals. *USA Today*'s international edition and the *International Herald Tribune* may be available at some hotels. For a real look at what's going on in the world, you may need to visit newsgathering Web sites. The government occasionally blocks or censors the BBC, but access to CNN and the *New York Times* is consistent. Local magazines that have up-to-date information on happenings around town include *Time Out Beijing*, *City Weekend* and *That's Beijing*.

PHOTO: TOR LINDQVIST/ISTOCKPHOTO

Currency

China's official currency, the renminbi (people's money), is often denoted as RMB and is generally synonymous with its main denomination, the yuan. Smaller denominations are the jiao (also called the mao) and the fen: 1 yuan = 10 jiao =100 fen. ATMs are available throughout the city. Be sure to notify your bank before you leave that you'll be traveling in China; some American banks are overzealous about account protection and will freeze your card the moment you try to use it in a Chinese ATM.

Rental Cars

Foreigners are not permitted to rent cars in Beijing, and this is a good thing. Navigating Beijing traffic is a hair-raising experience best left to the pros. Should you rent a car through a major international service like Avis or Hertz, a driver will come with the car, and an economy rental will cost between RMB750 and RMB850. Another option is hiring a taxi for the day. Negotiate the price but expect to pay between RMB300 and RMB600 for the service. Since most drivers do not speak English or read pinyin (the roman version of Mandarin words), it's essential to have your destinations written ahead of time in Mandarin characters, and make sure you have access to a cell phone in case your driver gets lost and needs to phone your destination for directions.

Weather

Beijing winters can be bone-achingly cold and dry (think Chicago in January when packing). Down parkas and warm boots are essential, as most tourist sites, including the Forbidden City and Temple of Heaven, are basically outdoor experiences. On the opposite extreme, Beijing summers can be hot and muggy with air pollution at its highest levels. Be aware that early spring brings sandstorms, which come in from central Asia and choke the city with swirling clouds of dust. Later spring and fall are ideal times to visit, with balmy days and fair temperatures.

Holidays

The annual spring holiday, or Chinese New Year, takes place around the first lunar cycle of the year. At this time, most Chinese leave the cities to return to their hometowns for a week's worth of celebration. This is a famously terrible time to travel in China, because flights, trains and buses are jammed to capacity with travelers. Other long holidays include Labor Day (May 1) and National Day (October 1), while the moon festival, or mid-autumn festival, usually takes place around mid-September.

Walking in Beijing

Crossing the street in Beijing can be an unexpected experience for foreigners. Cars are not required to stop (or slow down for that matter) before turning right on red and appear to have the right-of-way over pedestrians. Be vigilant for traffic coming at you from

PHOTO: TOR LINDQVIST/ISTOCKPHOTO

all directions, even when you have a green walk signal.

Scams

Unsuspecting tourists have reported falling victim to several scams around Beijing. These usually involve Western men being approached by Chinese women wanting to practice their English skills. The tourist is then invited to a tea ceremony, where several hours later a bill for as much as $400 for the tea is charged to the tourist's credit card. Other scams include invitations to art shows and other plans devised to separate tourists from their money. Avoid falling victim to scams by being skeptical of overly friendly over-

tures from locals—skip invitations that would divert you from your planned activities.

Medical matters

With its large foreign worker population, Beijing now has a number of decent Western-style medical facilities. The largest and most popular is United Family, a full-service hospital located near the Holiday Inn Lido hotel. It has a large number of American or U.S.-trained medical practitioners and specialists. Other facilities that may be more convenient for minor issues include International SOS, Bayley & Jackson Medical Center and the Hong Kong International Medical Clinic in the Swissôtel.

PHOTO: TOR LINDQVIST/ISTOCKPHOTO

Getting around via taxi

Most taxi drivers don't speak English (or understand the English names of places, including hotels), but you can still easily use them to get around. Have the doorman of the hotel provide the driver with instructions to your destination and make sure you keep a card with the hotel's name and address in Chinese.

Tipping rules

Tipping is not customary in China. It may feel awkward the first few times you "stiff" the waiter, driver or bellhop, but there are a few reasons why you really shouldn't tip. First, for some workers, it offends their sense of worker pride. Second, the tipping system in America doesn't exist in China—waiters are paid a salary that assumes no tips. While it may seem strange to you not to tip, to locals, tipping has about as much charm as someone reimbursing you for a gift.

Cell phones

The cellular network in China is, simply put, amazingly good. If you bring a GSM phone (the most popular standard for mobile phones), you will likely be able to use it. However, expect to pay fairly high international roaming rates from your domestic provider. The minute you get off the plane, you'll see

someone selling SIM cards. Resist the temptation to buy one. It probably won't work, since most mobile phones in the United States are subsidized by the carriers who "lock" the phone to their network. A number of places can safely "unlock" your phone from your carrier's network, allowing you to use any pay-as-you-go SIM card in China or anywhere else, but unless you plan to make local phone calls or be easily reachable by phone, it's usually not worth the hassle.

Local calls

Trying to make a local call can be a little confusing. In many cases, you can ask the concierge at the hotel to assist you. Beijing landlines are eight digits and mobile phones

PHOTO: LOIC BERNARD/iSTOCKPHOTO

throughout China are usually 11 digits, beginning with one or zero. There is no need to dial an area code for mobile phones, as all of China is under one system.

Finding a rest room

To ask for a rest room, you can gesture by rubbing your hands together and/or saying "Shee show jenn zai nar," which is a way of saying "Where is the hand washroom?" Most venues catering to foreigners will usually have Western-style facilities, but you may encounter the notorious "squatter" toilets in the public rest rooms at tourist destinations. These look like ceramic bedpans embedded in the floor and are challenging to those who have never used one. It's wise to carry your own tissue. Your best bet is to use the bathroom in your hotel and try not to drink too much water.

Taking the subway

Beijing has an excellent subway system that's expanding at an incredible pace. New lines are under construction connecting the Olympic Village to the city, and a planned airport-to-city center line is due to open this year. Grab a map and ask the hotel staff to identify the stops nearest to the places you would like to go. At the time of this writing, Beijing was transitioning from a simple one-fare model (of RMB2 per ticket) to variable amounts based upon the distance. Ticket vending machines are installed and ready for action, but if you are having trouble, you can always get help from an attendant at the window by showing him where you want to go. Station names are announced in Mandarin and English on the trains, and signage is also in both, making navigating the system simple.

Language

Mandarin is the official language in Beijing, and the romanized version of Mandarin words is called pinyin. Here are a few useful phrases:

Hello *Ni hao (nee how)*

How are you? *Ni hao ma (nee how ma)*

Thank you *Xie xie (sheh sheh)*

Goodbye *Zai jian (dzai jee-in)*

Sorry *Duibuqi (dwee boo chee)*

Please *Qing (ching)*

How much? *Duoshao (dor sheow)*

Yes *Shi (sher)*

No *Bu (boo)*

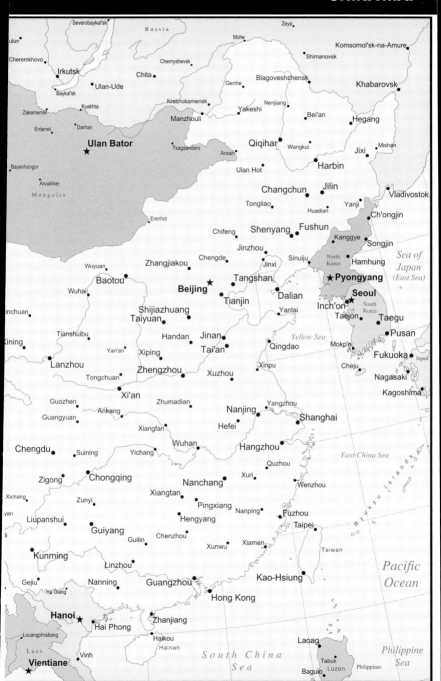

CHINA MAP

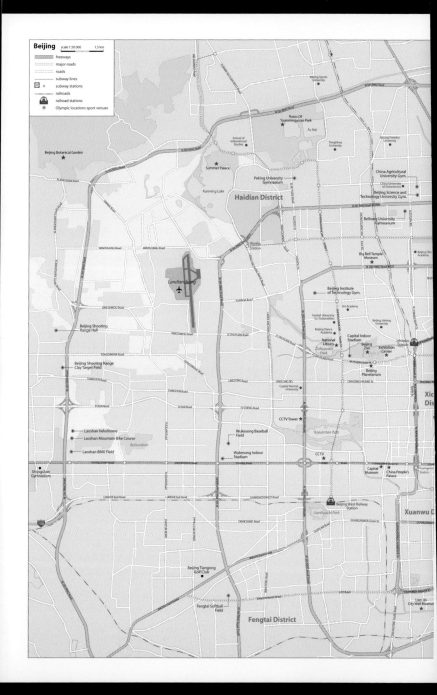

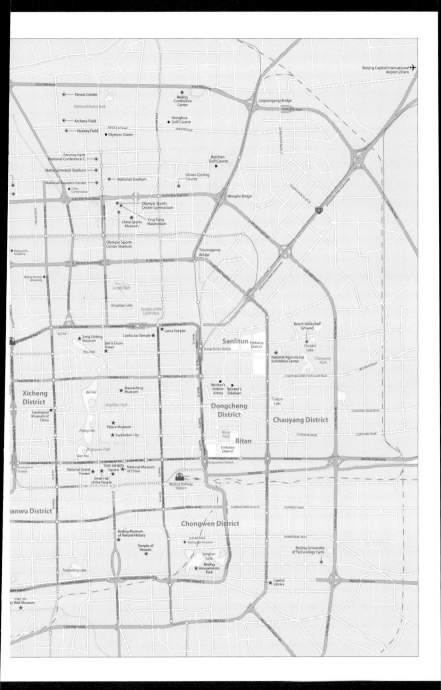

Beijing Capital International ✈
Airport 20 km

Tennis Center

National Forest Park

★ Beijing Conference Center

Laiguangying Bridge

Archery Field

● Honghua Golf Course

Hockey Field

● Olympic Green

Fencing Gym
National Conference C.

Beichen Golf Course

National Indoor Stadium

National Aquatics Center

★ National Stadium

Urban Cycling Course

● China Conservatory

Wanghe Bridge

Olympic Sports Center Gymnasium

● Beijing Film Academy

★ China Sports Museum

Ying Tung Natatorium

Beijing Normal University

Olympic Sports Center Stadium

Taiyanggong Bridge

Liuyin Park

Qingnian Lake

Temple of the Earth Park

Xi Hai

★ Song Qinling Museum

Bell & Drum Tower

Confucius Temple ★

★ Lama Temple

Sanlitun

Embassy District

Dongzhimen Station

Beach Volleyball Ground

Shuidui Lake

Chaoyang Park

Hou Hai

National Agricultural Exhibition Center

Xicheng District

Bei Hai

★ Maoredeng Museum

Worker's Indoor Arena

● Worker's Stadium

Tuanje Lake

Dongcheng District

Chaoyang District

Geological Museum of China ★

Jingshan Park

Zhong Hai

★ Palace Museum

★ Forbidden City

Ritan Park

Ritan

Embassy District

Nan Hai

Shijingshan Park

Jianguomen Station

★ National Grand Theater

TIAN ANMEN Square

National Museum of China

Great Hall of the People

Beijing Railway Station

...anwu District

Chongwen District

★ Beijing Museum of Natural History

YULAN Road

● Beijing Gymnasium

Longtan Lake

Temple of Heaven ★

★ Beijing Amusements Park

Beijing University of Technology Gym.

Taoranting Lake

...iao Jin
...ty Wall Museum

★ Capital Library

▶ BEIJING

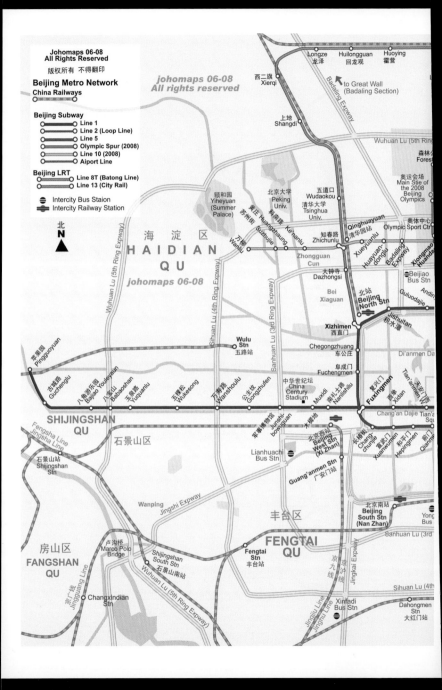

Beijing Metro Network
China Railways

Beijing Subway
Line 1
Line 2 (Loop Line)
Line 5
Olympic Spur (2008)
Line 10 (2008)
Aiport Line

Beijing LRT
Line 8T (Batong Line)
Line 13 (City Rail)

Intercity Bus Staion
Intercity Railway Station

北
N

海淀区
HAIDIAN
QU

johomaps 06-08

SHIJINGSHAN
QU
石景山区

房山区
FANGSHAN
QU

丰台区
FENGTAI
QU

Longze 龙泽
Huilongguan 回龙观
Huoying 霍营

西二旗 Xierqi

to Great Wall (Badaling Section)

Shangdi 上地

Wuhuan Lu (5th Ring)

森林公园 Forest

颐和园 Yiheyuan (Summer Palace)

北京大学 Peking Univ.
清华大学 Tsinghua Univ.
五道口 Wudaokou
知春路 Zhichunlu

奥运会场 Main Stie of the 2008 Beijing Olympics

黄庄 Huangzhuang
科南街 Kenanlu
苏州街 Suzhoujie
万柳 Wanliu

Qinghuayuan 清华园站

奥体中心 Olympic Sport Ctr

中关村 Zhongguan Cun
大钟寺 Dazhongsi

Xueyuanlu 学院路
Huayuan-dongli 花园东里
Badaling Expway

Xiongmao Huandao 熊猫环岛

北站 Beijing North Stn
Beijiao Bus Stn
Andin
Guluodajie 鼓楼大街

Bei Xiaguan 北下关

Xizhimen 西直门
Jishuitan 积水潭

Chegongzhuang 车公庄
Di'anmen Da

Fuchengmen 阜成门
阜成门

五路站 Wulu Stn

中华世纪坛 China Century Stadium
Muxidi 木樨地
复兴门 Fuxingmen
Nanlishilu 南礼士路

Tian'anmen
天安门
西单 Xidan

萍果园 Pingguoyuan
古城路 Guchenglu
八角游乐园 Bajiao Youleyuan
八宝山 Babaoshan
玉泉路 Yuquanlu
五棵松 Wukesong
万寿路 Wanshoulu
公主坟 Gongzhufen

Chang'an Dajie Tian'
Chang'an Dajie

Chang-chunjie 长椿街
Xuanwumen 宣武门
Hepingmen 和平门
Qianmen 前门

Fengsha Line 丰沙线
Jingsha Line

石景山站 Shijingshan Stn

Lianhuachi Bus Stn 莲花池

北京西站 Beijing West Stn (Xi Zhan)

军事博物馆 Junshi bowuguan

北京南站 Beijing South Stn (Nan Zhan)

Wanping 卢沟桥 Marco Polo Bridge

Jingshi Expway

Guang'anmen Stn 广安门站

北京南站 Beijing South Stn (Nan Zhan)

Yong Bus

京广线 Jingguang Line

Shijingshan South Stn 石景山南站

Fengtai Stn 丰台站

Sanhuan Lu (3rd

京九线 Jingjiu Line
Jingkai Expway

Changxindian Stn 长辛店站

Sihuan Lu (4th

Xinfadi Bus Stn 新发地

Dahongmen Stn 大红门站

158 www.mobiltravelguide.com

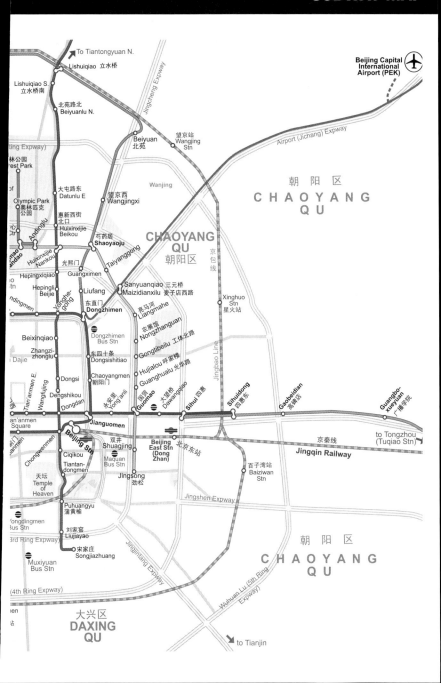

Colorful Chinese umbrellas

An Olympic tribute

Crimson wall of the Forbidden City

Bicycles, a primary mode of transportation

PHOTO-KINABALOO.COM

Chinese lanterns

PHOTO: MICHAEL BONACCI

NOTES

NOTES